The Arts Council

Photo-Realism
Paintings, sculpture and prints
from the Ludwig Collection and others

4 April-6 May 1973

Serpentine Gallery

Printed in England by Shenval

Preface

This exhibition — the first in this country to represent the new realist trend in the United States — is also the first Serpentine exhibition not devoted to the work of young British artists. Heating has been installed, we can plan a more or less year-round season, and so we decided to vary the programme. The art of the young and the relatively unknown will continue to occupy the time and space it did and possibly more, but the Serpentine will also present shows that focus on varying themes, media, countries and individuals of current interest.

Photo-Realism is one of the names given to the work of several young painters and a few sculptors, first in America (there was a seminal show at Vassar College in 1968) and now more internationally. Last year's *Documenta* exhibition at Kassel, intended to illustrate differing concepts of reality in contemporary art, included a large and convincing section devoted to this kind of painting and sculpture. Meanwhile books and articles have been assembled to give an initially controversial phenomenon the respectability of recognized avant-garde status.

How radical the new realism is, or how reactionary and even materialistic, is still open to continuing debate. We should like only to stress that the more a work of art looks like a photograph, the more misleading it will be to encounter it only in the form of photographs and reproductions. It is more than ever essential to confront the actual object, to assess scale, colour, texture. In other words, what else went into the work?

Dr Peter Ludwig is now world famous as a collector. Cologne and Aachen are honoured to house great parts of his collection, and it is from the latter that we have been permitted to draw the dominant part of this exhibition. We are deeply grateful to Dr Ludwig for this, and salute him as one of those rare collectors whose activity makes a positive contribution to our awareness and understanding of contemporary art. Dr Wolfgang Becker, charged with the care of the Neue Galerie im Alten Kurhaus and with that part of the Ludwig collection housed there, has been of continuous assistance to us and we have benefited from his advice. It was especially considerate of Dr Ludwig and Dr Becker to permit us to add some loans from other sources, in Britain and in the United States, to round out our exhibition in one or two respects, and we are very grateful to those other lenders who were willing to be used in this way.

Dr Brigitte Lohmeyer of the German Embassy and Dr Klaus Schulz of the German Institute in London, also the United States Information Service, helped us in several important respects, and we have enjoyed unfailing cooperation from Mr K W Jensen of the Louisiana Museum near Copenhagen where a larger range of works from Dr Ludwig's collection was recently on show.

Robin Campbell, *Director of Art*
Norbert Lynton, *Director of Exhibitions*

Introduction

The discovery of the usefulness of photographs to a special form of realist painting began ten years ago. Richard Artschwager made a series of monochromes in which washes of liquitex, spread across a porous board, built up grainy images of buildings and other subjects, the veracity of which was a cross-between newsprint and Daguerre. Malcolm Morley did several naval subjects in a similar monochrome before beginning in 1965 his fully polychromatic paintings of ocean liners, followed by cabin interiors. Artschwager has continued his monochromatic images, staying close to his initial style, but the work in this exhibition is concentrated on the simulation of colour photography rather than black-and-white. The choice of work presumes an equivocal correlation between the status of painting and the photographic source, which means that Morley's later works, photographically derived but translated in terms of an unruly dark-keyed painterliness are excluded. What is presented here are the painters of a bright sunlit world or, at least, of bright sunlit photographs.

A few names have been proposed for this kind of painting, none of which questions its status as a form of realism. There is new realism, which overlaps too many old new realisms, to be useful. There is radical realism which has the disadvantage of originating with a dealer, thus mixing the functions of promotion and criticism. The same qualification must be attached to sharp-focus realism, a term which, whatever its origin, has been compromised by dealer use. Or there is photo-realism, adopted for this exhibition, which uses a contraction meaning photographic. I shall spell it out here as photographic realism and mean by it paintings that pertain to photography and are 'suggestive of a photograph' (Random House Dictionary, unabridged).

In England the use of photographs by artists is not new: there is Sickert's well-known portrait of King George V and there is the extensive use of momentary poses and blurred forms in Francis Bacon's work. Peter Blake derived figure paintings from magazine pin-ups at an early date, too. However, the thorough simulation of photographs or photographic reproductions by hand-done paintings is less familiar and it is this practice that has developed in the United States in the last ten years. There is no doubt: Pop art was influential here, whether as a model of admitting casual contemporary subject matter or of imitating in paintings images characterized by other means of communication. Warhol's use of repetitive photographs and Rauschenberg's use of a proliferation of photographs in their silkscreened paintings shows, within the terms of Pop art, an interest in annexing ready-made imagery and in simulating other channels.

The first exhibitions of photographic realism[1] combined Artschwager and Morley with Rauschenberg and Warhol on the basis of their common photographic sources. Though distinctions emerged later, the origin of photographic realism close to Pop art is significant for it enables us to define one aspect of the tendency with some confidence. What happens when an artist quotes a photograph, not simply as an *aide memoire* as Delacroix and Courbet did, but in such a way that the photographic quality as well as the depicted object are readable in the painting? To answer this we can define a photograph as a system of co-incident 'points between the photograph and pre-existing points of physical reality'.[2] For this reason, as William M Ivins Jr has pointed out, 'a photograph is today accepted as proof of the existence of things and shapes that never would have been believed on the evidence of a hand-made picture'.[3] In this sense, the photographic realist can count on the evidential content of photographs, reliable to him as a source of visual data

and trusted by the spectators who share his belief in the medium. The photographic sources can be found or newly made: found sources include Morley's travel poster ektachromes and McLean's ads in ranch and stable magazines; newly made sources include Bechtle's, Goings', and Parrish's own photographs, taken with a view to being painted later. There is not all that difference between them, because personal photographs easily take on the standard gloss of cinemascope movies, colour ads in weekly magazines and display effects in automobile or kitchen appliance literature.

One of the reasons for the believability of photographic reproduction is the fact that, to quote Ivins again, 'the lines of the process . . . could be below the threshold of normal human vision'.[5] Hence it was 'a way of making visual reports that had no interfering symbolic linear syntax of their own'.[6] Compared to the engravings (Ivins' 'linear syntax') that preceded photography as a method of reproducing objects, this is quite true but, in addition, there have been consumers and producers of photography for generations now. Thus along with the credibility of photographs is the fact that we have enveloped an expertise that makes us aware of the limits of the process itself. Cropping, focus, and omitted material are a part of photographic conventions as well as the iconicity of the image. Thus photography has acquired its syntax too, its specific channel characteristics. As a result, when we look at a photographic realist painting there is a double image: we see both a painting and an image clearly derived from a photograph. The painting carries a reference to another channel of communication as well as to the depicted scene or object. The reality of photographs, however, is not the reality of slow, hand-done paintings, so that the realism of the subject matter is definitely called in doubt. It is as if the subject matter of, say, Eddy's picture is not a Volkswagen but a photograph of a Volkswagen. The photograph corresponds to the car as we know it, but the painting corresponds as much to the photograph as to the car; it is, perhaps, the photograph that functions as the primary reference. To the extent that this is so the terms photographic and realism can be viewed centrifugally, as tearing themselves apart by the interplay of channel and iconography.[6]

The artists are of course all concerned with the illusionism that accompanies high finish in the rendering of stable objects and scenes. The style does not, for the most part, refer to things in use, but to things on display, for sale it seems. By taking the lustrous surfaces of Hollywood photography and Detroit styling as norms, the artists have cultivated a deceptive realism. There is a sustained sense of newness, of a world of highlights that is stylistically akin to the ravishing reflections and gradations in, say, brochures for new cars or company reports on new products. This means that the realism of these artists is diverted from its expected target, turned away from the notion of use in the world and the occupancy of real space and affiliated with the sphere of symbolic use, of advertising. The rhetoric of consumer persuasion is attached to the finish of these pictures, a point made not in criticism but descriptively. It is by adopting the impact of the imagery of commercial art that the photographic realists present their imagery so forcefully. It is their irony, and one cultivated by the artists to judge from their evasive remarks on iconography quoted in the catalogue, that the technique does not enshrine the object so much as define its periphery of symbolic uses in the media.

Consider some representative statements[7] concerning iconography and the artists' attitudes towards it. Bechtle 'I am certainly aware of the social implications of my subjects, but I try to preserve a kind of neutrality', Cottingham 'I'm just using the subject as the stepping-off point to compose the subject'. Eddy 'I think the subject matter is dictated to me by the kind of painting problems I'm interested in'. McLean 'I think neutrality is extremely important' and Morley has always equivocated about his engagement in the iconography of his paintings. None of the artists expresses, as a realist would, his commitment to objects or a situation in the world. On the contrary, they stress stances either of detachment or formal convenience.

It was the intention of the organizers of *documenta 5*, the exhibition held at Kassel last summer, to compare American photographic realism with Soviet social realism.[8] In the event only the American contingent was shown, but the project was clearly based on an iconographical reading of the works involved. What is characteristic of the photographic realists, but the topography of the interfaces and points-of-sale of American life? Leisure subjects include ocean liners and prize horses, beach scenes and movie stars' homes. There are street scenes with the web of reflections that was unknown to urban life before the twentieth century (the Futurists and Léger were the first to notice the effect of the use of glass in the city) and fascias signalling wares and services. Cars are present in a complete cycle from show room to car park, from street parking lot to wrecking yard. Highway culture is present from gleaming capacious trailer to gleaming customized motor cycle. Thus there is a subject matter of great accessibility, not only to Americans who recognize the details of the hardware but to Europeans who recognize the process of industrialization that makes all this possible and who know their equivalents. Compared to Soviet realism, which is closely related to genre and history painting, American photographic realism derives from its source a sense of chance configurations at arrested moments. Russian realism aims to mould images that are historically significant whereas the American artists aim at the statistically familiar. There is in this kind of painting a discrepancy that produces a formal tension between the high finish of the paintings as objects and the typical, randomly chosen subjects that they depict.

There is obviously no built-in restriction in the subject matter of photographic realism, but Morley is one of the few to have dealt with the past in his chateau and castle pictures (begun on the basis of a postcard that David Hockney sent him). However, it is significant that the iconography of these painters includes a minimum of historical references; what they seem engaged with is the typicality of the present, the conjunctions of objects that are normal in our society, not its precious monuments.[9] A great many of the scenes and objects that they represent, such as Goings' Airstream trailer or Salt's cars are meaningful to us by their commonness. This is no less true of Close's portraits than of the other artists' objects, inasmuch as they are selected from the artists' friends and are representative of the art world in terms of social style and type. This use of a fund of common images and signs is related to Pop art. The statements by the artists quoted in the catalogue include in only a single case a response to a question on the subject which all the artists were asked originally. McLean is alone with his 'Sure, I owe a big debt to Pop'. However, the other painters have recorded various degrees of affection or obligation.[10] Goings is especially interesting in this context, when he says: 'I believe in a kind of random order in the way reality puts itself together'.[11] The oxymoron random order was coined by Rauschenberg who used it, as Goings does, to describe the chance conjunctions of daily life.[12]

What we have therefore in photographic realism is an art of high visual impact, but with complexities held in suspense within it.

There is no single and direct route from the signifier to the signified. It is true that this iconography is derived from everyday life. To quote Henri Lefevbre 'the quotidian is what is humble and solid, what is taken for granted and that of which all the parts follow each other in such a regular succession that those concerned have no call to question their sequence'.[13] However, as we have seen the quotidian is not directly expressed in these paintings. It is mediated by borrowed images, by the quotation of sources known, at least in type, to the spectators as well as to the artists. Thus there is an intricate relation of the painting as one kind of sign to other signs of an absent object, but a sign which, owing to the technique of presentation, appears as a powerful presence. To borrowed images and mediated references we must add the emotional disengagement of the artists, for which we have their own word. This complex situation, an interplay of illusion and convention in deceptive intimacies, the disinvolvement from passion'[14], is as reminiscent of Mannerism as of realism. Such a view seems to accord with the fascinating mixture of daily subjects oddly distanced from us, of complex references rather than substantial presences, that characterize photographic realism.

Lawrence Alloway, New York, 1973

Notes

1 In 1964 an exhibition, *The Painter and the Photograph,* University of New Mexico, Albuquerque, arranged by Van Deren Coke, surveyed the whole field. In 1966 *The Photographic Image,* Solomon R Guggenheim Museum, NYC, arranged by the author, included painters Richard Artschwager, Lynn Foulkes, Malcolm Morley and Joseph Raffaele (as he then was), collagist Suzi Gablik, and silkscreen printers Rauschenberg and Warhol. In 1969 *Paintings from the Photo,* Riverside Museum, NY, arranged by Oriole Farb, showed only painters: Harold Brider, Richard Estes, Audrey Flack, Howard Kanovitz, Malcolm Morley and Raffael (as his name now was). The direct printing of photographs was excluded and the manual act of transcription had become central.

2 Max Bense, *Aesthetics and Photograph,* Camera 4, 1958 — English summary

3 William M Ivins Jr, *Prints and Visual Communications,* London 1953, p 94

4 Ibid pp 176–7

5 Ibid

6 It is this aspect of photographic realism, its conversion of channel to subject matter, that lead to its being called Post Pop art (see the author's *Art as Likeness,* Arts Magazine, 41/7 May 1967, pp 34–39). Note that Roy Lichtenstein's comic strip imagery simulates another channel of information as well as an appropriated image.

7 *The Photo-Realists: 12 Interviews,* Art in America, November/December 1972, pp 73–89

8 For a list of the projected Soviet representation, see the author's *'Reality': Ideology at D5,* Artforum, 11 October 1972, p 36.

9 Aside from Morley, Audrey Flack, with her paintings of Macarenza Esperanza (a seventeenth century statue), Notre Dame and Michelangelo's David, has dealt with the image of historic monuments filtered by modern slide technology.

10 See Art in America, Op Cit. The statements in the present catalogue are from this source, but the artists' responses to a question about Pop art have not been reprinted. Bechtle: 'Pop was the catalyst' (p 74). Close: 'Certainly we have to be aware of the fact that Pop happened' (p 76). Cottingham: 'Pop showed us that there was a lot more subject matter around than we were paying attention to' (p 78). Eddy: 'Without Pop I don't think this would have happened' (p 81). Estes: 'I always liked Pop' (p 79). Salt: 'I like some of the Pop artists, sure, but it's a long way away' (p 88).

11 Ibid p 88

12 Robert Rauschenberg, *Random Order,* Location 1/1 1963, pp 27–31

13 Henri Lefebvre, *Everyday Life in the Modern World,* translation by Sacha Rabinovitch, New York 1971, p 24

14 John Shearman, *Mannerism,* Harmondsworth 1967, p 61

John de Andrea

Born in Denver, Colorado in 1941. Studied at University of Colorado
1962–65. Lives in Denver.

One-man exhibitions 1970, 1971 O K Harris, NYC; 1971 Wilamaro
Art Gallery, Denver

Some group exhibitions 1971 *Radical Realism,* Museum of Contemporary Art, Chicago; *VII Biennale des Jeunes Artistes,* Paris;
New Realism, Old Realism, Danenberg & Roman, Contemporaries
Inc, NYC; 1972 *Sharp-Focus Realism,* Sidney Janis Gallery, NYC;
documenta 5, Kassel; 1973 *Ekstrem realisme,* Louisiana Museum
of Modern Art, Humlebaek

1　**Dorothy**　1969/70　*illustrated*
fibreglass 170 x 70 x 40
Ludwig Collection, Neue Galerie, Aachen

Sizes are given in centimetres, height before width

How 'real' do you want your figures to be?
I want them to breathe.
How important is the painting of your sculpture?
I treat a colour as loose as possible. There are so many things going
on under the skin and if you try to control it too much you can't
get as much variation. In the underpainting, I treat the extremities,
especially the legs, like something containing blood. I splash on that
blood red almost like an abstract painting, then wash and push
it with my hands and build it up until the legs get purplish. As
I paint the skin and start working down I start using more of the
blood and purple. I can make the brush do just as well as a spray
gun, and all that red underpainting makes you keep inventing as
you go. I've studied skin colours and a lot of complexion differences,
and I try to paint those differences. I like to feel I'm inventing with
paint, and I always set up challenges with paint. I never save my
palette but try to invent a whole new one every time I make a new
figure. After two or three years I'll add a few colours to it. I split
them down real fine — so fine that at the end of the day I'll think
I've got a certain shade of red. Then I'll walk away and come back
the next day, and I can't even find the thing. That's how fine I split
the colours.
**The critical reaction to New Realism, and to the kind of work
you're doing, has been quite negative. Some critics feel there
is simply too much technical rhetoric.**
The technical aspects are important to me because in order to make
the figures breathe you have to work on that technique, but you
treat it separately. It's not like you back up and say, boy did I kid
somebody into something. The back on a new standing figure I've
just completed is so real that you'd swear to Christ she's breathing.
It astounded me. It scared me. Now that's the beauty of it. The
viewer can't talk to these figures, but he can do a lot of judging. He
can like or dislike the figures. He can be repulsed or fall in love with
them. I'm after this response. It's all I have to work with, and that's
why I keep my surface so immaculate. I try to tell about the person
just from that surface.
Is your world an ideal world?
I set up my own world, and it is a very peaceful world — at least my
sculptures are. There is a lot of quietness in those figures, and
they're meant to be seen separately. Hanson shows a lot of the gore
that is associated with the 'real world', but a lot of the New Realists
don't show that. They have a very passive world like mine. It's just
a piece of life. It's not a rocket ship, but it's like looking out of a
window and taking a small chunk of life.

from an interview by Duncan Pollock, *Art in America*, Nov/Dec 1972

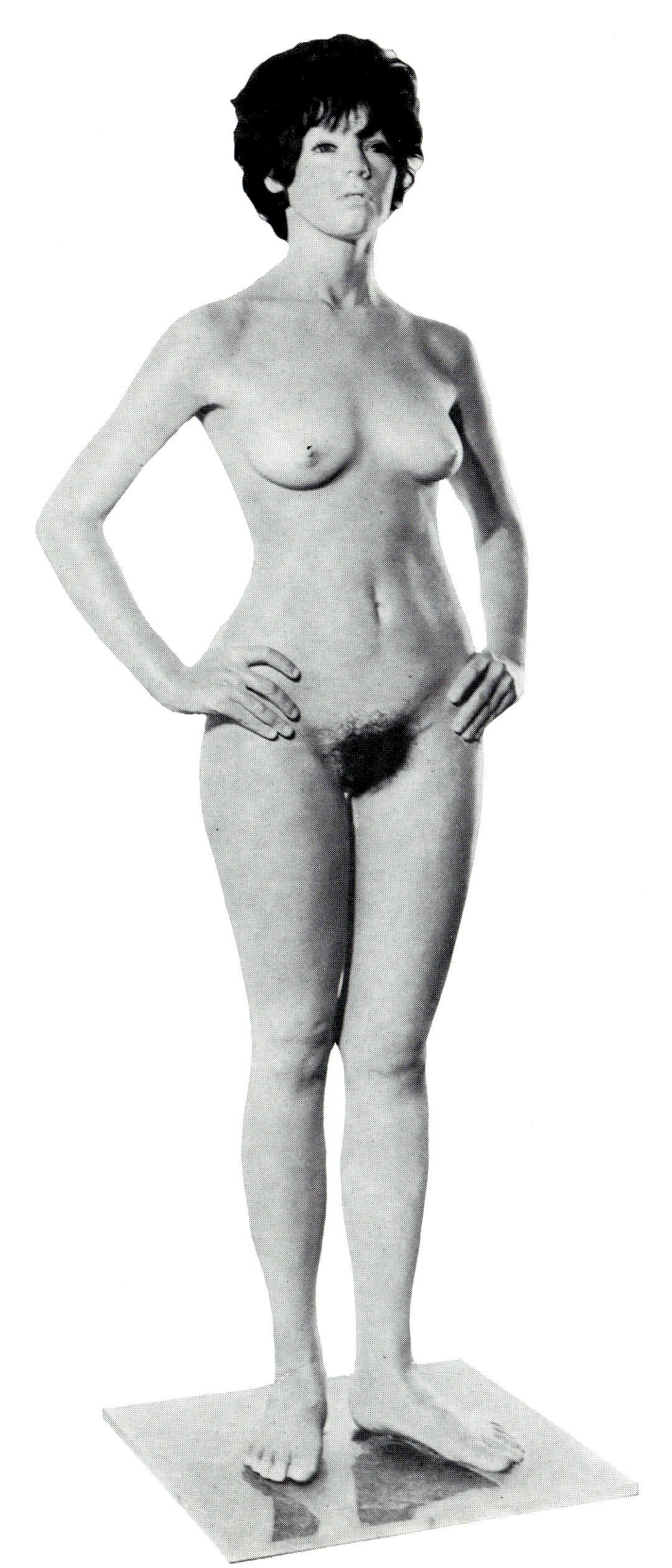

Robert Bechtle

Born in San Francisco in 1932. Studied at California College of Arts and Crafts and University of California, Berkeley 1955–58. Taught at University of California, Berkeley 1965–66 and Davis 1967–68. Since 1969 has lived in San Francisco and taught at California College of Arts and Crafts and San Francisco State College.

One-man exhibitions 1959, 1964, 1967 San Francisco Museum of Art; 1965 Richmond Art Center, California; 1965, 1967 Berkeley Gallery, San Francisco; 1966 Crocker Art Gallery, Sacramento; 1967 University of California, Davis; 1969 Achenbach Foundation for Graphic Arts, San Francisco; 1971 O K Harris, NYC

Some group exhibitions 1966 *Eastbay Realists,* San Francisco Art Institute; 1968 *Realism Now,* Vassar College Art Gallery, NY; 1969 *Aspects of a New Realism,* Milwaukee Art Center, Wisconsin; 1969 *The American Realist Tradition,* University of Oklahoma, Tulsa; 1970 *22 Realists,* Whitney Museum of American Art, NYC; *The Highway Show,* Institute of Contemporary Art, Philadelphia; 1971 *The Cool Realists,* Jack Glenn Gallery, Corona del Mar, California; *Radical Realism,* Museum of Contemporary Art, Chicago; *New Realism,* State University at Potsdam, NY; *The Shape of Realism,* Deson Zaks Gallery, Chicago; 1972 *documenta 5,* Kassel; *Phases of New Realism,* Lowe Art Museum, Coral Gables, Florida; 1972/73 *Amerikanischer Fotorealismus,* Württembergischer Kunstverein, Frankfurter Kunstverein, Kunst-und Museumsverein, Wuppertal; 1973 *Ekstrem realisme,* Louisiana Museum of Modern Art, Humlebaek

2 Date Palms 1970/71 *illustrated*
oil on canvas 152 x 214
Ludwig Collection, Neue Galerie, Aachen

3 68 Nova
lithograph 65 x 91 from *10 documenta super realists* portfolio edition of 300, published by Shorewood Atelier, NYC, edition of 300
Arts Council Collection

How do you feel about being included in the Neo-Realist or Photo-Realist group?
We are not really a group; we're all doing individual things. Until recently there was so little significant realist painting compared to abstract painting that it was very easy to group the realists under a label as if they were working toward common goals. So people would tend to be thrown together as realists when, philosophically, they were quite far apart.
Most of us made a personal decision that what had been happening in painting was relatively closed off to us, that too many people had there been before us and that there were too many predictables. Realism became a way of getting away from that in the sense that you didn't feel the ground was already broken. That sounds strange, since realism seems so traditional. Yet, when you think of it, the real tradition today is modernism, and it is now almost one century old.

Is New Realism a reactionary occasion?
I don't think so. It's not avant-garde in the way we've come to understand the term, but it's not reactionary in the sense of trying to go back someplace. I don't think it attempts to maintain the old realist tradition in any way. Quite the contrary. A lot of abstract art is present in what we're doing.

What's your attitude toward photography?
It's complicated. I try to think of it as a tool. That's how I started using it, to enable me to paint things that I couldn't paint otherwise.

You can't very well paint a car by setting your easel up on the street for three months. But of course the use of photographs starts to affect the way you think and see too. It can't really be just a tool.

How does the photograph affect your way of thinking?
I found for example, that I was allowing the way I would crop with the camera to affect the way I was cropping paintings. I felt I had to pull away from it and back off to what I thought was a less photographic kind of format.

Does the photograph push you into areas you didn't want to go to?
There's a lot of danger there. The danger of making finished photographs, for one. I have to be careful that they are really lousy photographs that will allow the completion to take place in the painting. If the photograph is too good and can stand as a finished work of art by itself, there is no reason to make a painting from it. I also feel I must try to avoid a too candid kind of photography; it's very easy for that quality to creep in when using a 35mm camera.
A photograph often gives the feeling of a particular moment in time, and you get the sense of how that is bracketed in with the before and after. I like the kind of photograph that tends to just be. You sense that what came before was exactly the same as what is shown, and that what comes next is going to be exactly the same. It is a kind of extension of time, which is a very traditional aspect of painting.

Do you have an attitude toward the state of time that photographs present?
I suppose my attitude has to do with a fairly traditional notion of what manner of time and motion is proper to painting. There are a lot of things you can photograph in motion, for instance, which make sense as a photograph but which become false in a painting because painting is essentially a static art. I try to find and use that particular static quality to advantage, to make something happen, perhaps, that doesn't happen in a photograph.

Is the all-overness of New Realism an important part of it — spending as much time on a patch of sky as on the face?
Yes. Because the sky is just as important a component of that surface as what is done in the face. Each area, at least in theory, has to receive an equal amount of attention. Of course you may spend more time and energy painting the face than you will painting the sky, but that shouldn't show when the painting is finished. It also has to do with a desire to avoid editorialising about the relative importance of the objects in the painting.

That goes back to that neutrality. You feel strongly about leaving it open.
I find it fascinating that I can paint something which is very specific — a particular car or a particular person at an identifiable location — that is just as open to various interpretations as an abstract painting.

When you talk about leaving it open and feeling strongly about it at the same time, that brings you into the precincts of the great classical tradition, doesn't it — Ingres, David, Vermeer?
I'm very conscious of Vermeer, of course. I also admire Degas and Winslow Homer and Edward Hopper.

from an interview by Brian O'Doherty, *Art in America*, Nov/Dec 1972

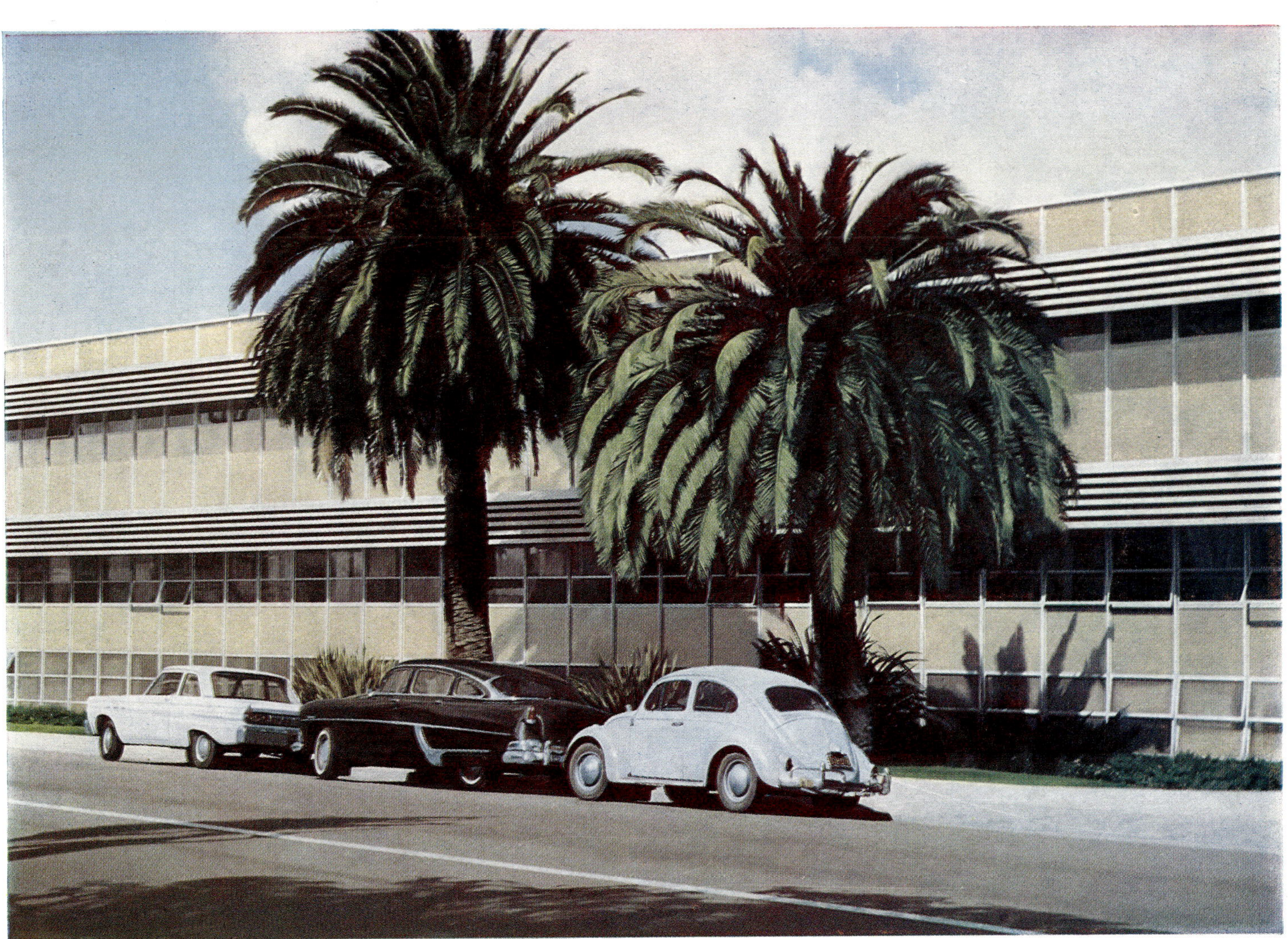

Chuck Close

Born in Monroe, Washington in 1940. Studied at Everett Community College, Washington 1958–60, University of Washington School of Art, Seattle 1960-62 and Yale School of Art & Architecture, Yale University, New Haven 1962–64; awarded a Fulbright Scholarship to study in Vienna 1964–65. Taught at University of Massachusetts School of Art, Amherst 1965–67. Since 1967 has lived in New York and up to 1971 taught at the School of Visual Arts.

One-man exhibitions 1967 University of Massachusetts Art Gallery, Amherst; 1970, 1971 Bykert Gallery, NYC; 1971 Los Angeles County Museum of Art; 1972 Museum of Contemporary Art, Chicago

Some group exhibitions 1970 *22 Realists,* Whitney Museum of American Art, NYC; *Three Young Americans,* Allen Memorial Art Museum, Oberlin College, Ohio; 1972 *Gigantic Scale,* Sidney Janis Gallery, NYC; *documenta 5,* Kassel; 1972/73 *Amerikanischer Fotorealismus,* Wurttembergischer Kunstverein, Frankfurter Kunstverein, Kunst-und Museumsverein, Wuppertal; 1973 *Ekstrem realisme,* Louisiana Museum of Modern Art, Humlebaek

4   **Richard**   1969   *illustrated*
(Portrait of artist Richard Serra)
acrylic on canvas 274 x 213
Ludwig Collection, Neue Galerie, Aachen

5   **Nat**   1972
watercolour on paper 173 x 142
Ludwig Collection, Neue Galerie, Aachen

You have made a certain attempt to dissociate yourself from New Realism, for example, by not being in the Sharp-Focus Realism show at the Sidney Janis Gallery. Why is this?
I have nothing against New Realism, but I'm not interested in attaching myself to a movement, which I don't think exists anyway. I have very personal reasons for making the paintings I make. I didn't set out to make New Realist paintings. My paintings are a result of certain self-imposed restrictions that I set up for myself. Painting a figure, painting an image, is just one viable alternative.

How did you start making these paintings?
I was really disgusted with the paintings I'd been making, and I was really disgusted with my education – because I'd been such a good student, and to be a good student you have to be a performing artist. You know what you can do and you are rewarded for it. I'd been told that I had a 'good hand' – which basically meant I made good art marks. My hand moves in ways that made these art marks quite easily, and I could imitate other people's art marks, so what I made was art. The other thing I was told was that I had 'a good sense of colour', whatever that is. I guess it means that I know magenta and red don't clash. So for a long time my paintings were full of personal cliché marks, very eclectic and full of these pat colour solutions. So I just stopped. Made a clear break. I decided I didn't want to make those paintings anymore; I wanted to do something different, to force myself to make new solutions. So, I decided to work from photographs, not because that's what I wanted my art to be about, but because no matter how interesting a shape was, if it wasn't in the photograph I couldn't use it.

So you consciously made yourself into a different kind of painter?
Yes. It wasn't that what I was doing was not me, but that it was only one aspect of the things I was thinking about. And since it had become so habitual, even the strongest things about my work were tainted by the lazy habitual things. It seemed better to get rid of it all.

How do you choose the subject matter?
I paint my friends because they put up with it. The reason I use a head instead of a tree is that I'm a lazy person and would tend to let myself get by with things. If the colour was slightly off or the texture of the bark of a tree was wrong, who would know? Who cares enough about trees to notice? I would not be as tough on myself when it comes to certain colour problems, etc. People are important to other people, so they're important to me. Also, likeness is a by-product of the way I work. Another reason I use my friends instead of a totally anonymous photograph is that it would really bother me if it didn't come out right. It would bother me even more if I did a lousy job of translating the photograph of someone I know.

Are you interested in reproducing the photograph?
I am trying to make it very clear that I am making paintings from photographs and that this is not the way the human eye sees it. If I stare at this it's sharp, and if I stare at that it's sharp too. The eye is very flexible, but the camera is a one-eye view of the world, and I think we know what a blur looks like only because of photography. It really nailed down blur. It's this elusive thing, and the camera gives you the information that was too difficult to deal with otherwise.

Why did you start the colour paintings?
After a while with the black and white paintings I began to get into cliché marks again, so I decided to change the problem. But I didn't want to change everything, so I decided I would alter one variable and try colour. The minimum number of colours to get full colour is three, so I had the transfers made and started trying colour. I used to have five or six favourite colours that I would use. Now I use three colours and I have to use all three. I can't prefer one to the other. Every square inch has some of all three. One result is that I'm mixing colours I never made in my life. I find it very liberating to accept things from the start as the eventual issues in the painting.

Some people would think of that as more restricting than liberating.
Right, but every limitation I have made has just opened things up and made it much more possible to make decisions. When everything in the world was a possibility I only tried three things or four things over and over. It's true. It's incredible. I didn't take advantage of that supposed freedom, and once I decided I was going to have relatively severe limitations, everything opened up; I have the possibility of making decisions about things other than how I feel on a certain day etc. I was never happy inventing interesting shapes and interesting colour combinations because all I could think of was how other people had done it. I couldn't get other people out of my paintings because the only solutions were the ones that were already nailed down. Now there is no invention at all; I simply accept the subject matter. I accept the situation. There is still invention. It's a different kind of invention. It's 'how to do it', and I find that, as a kind of invention, much more interesting. I do think approaching a painting that way – with any kind of self-imposed discipline – ultimately affects the subject matter. That's what sustains me. I'm not concerned with painting people or with making humanist paintings.

from an interview by Linda Chase and Ted McBurnett, *Art in America,* Nov/Dec 1972

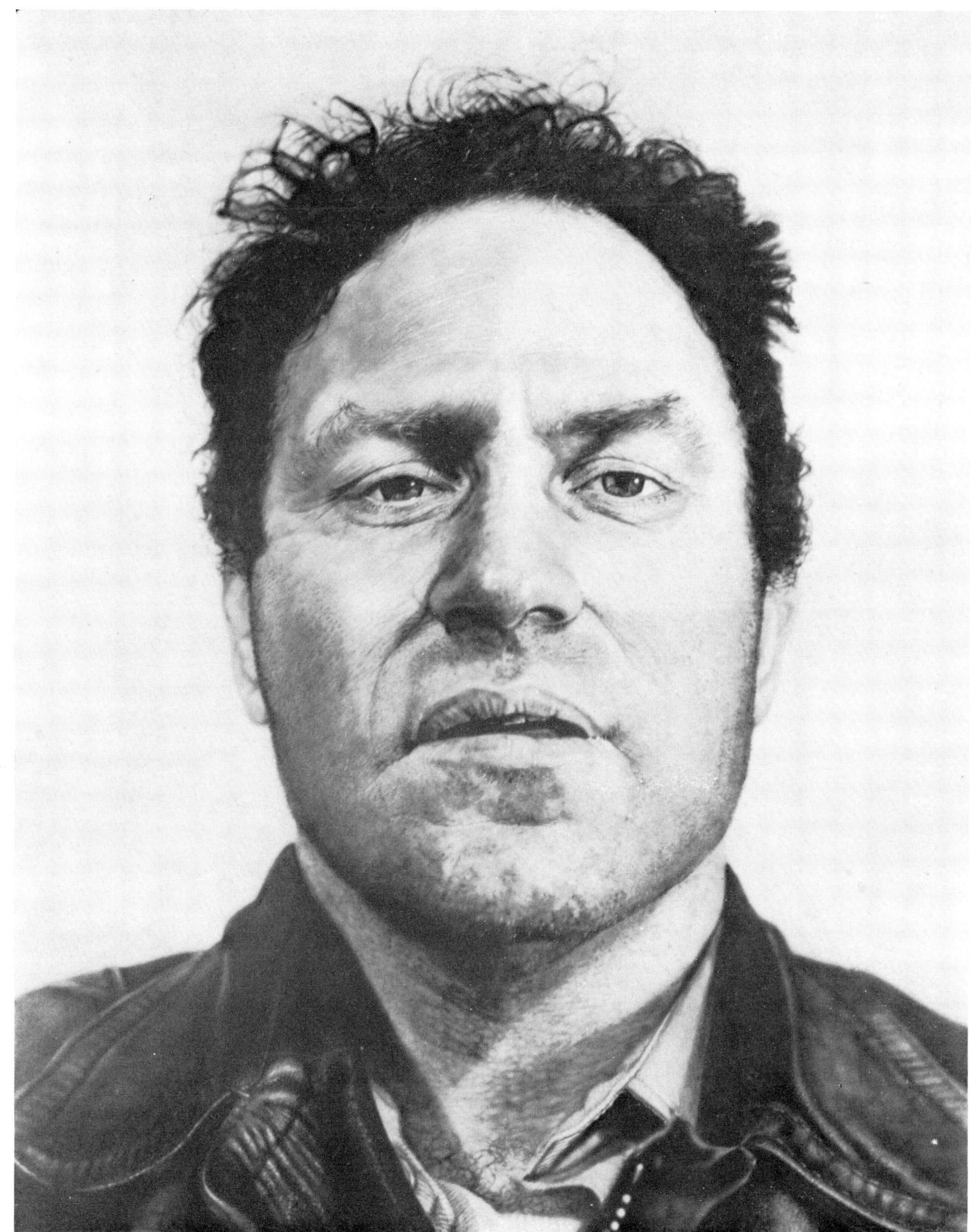

Robert Cottingham

Born in Brooklyn, New York in 1935. Studied at Pratt Institute, Brooklyn. Taught at Art Center College of Design 1969–70. At present lives in London

One-man exhibitions 1968, 1969 1970 Molly Barnes Gallery, Los Angeles; 1971 O K Harris, NYC

Some group exhibitions 1968 *The California Landscape,* Lytton Savings and Loan, Los Angeles; 1970 *The Persistent Image,* Fresno State College, California; *The Highway Show,* Institute of Contemporary Art, Philadelphia; 1971 *Radical Realism,* Museum of Contemporary Art, Chicago; *New Realism,* State University at Potsdam, NY; 1972 *Sharp-Focus Realism,* Sidney Janis Gallery, NYC; *documenta 5,* Kassel; 1972/73 *Amerikanischer Fotorealismus,* Württembergischer Kunstverein, Frankfurter Kunstverein, Kunst -und Museumsverein, Wuppertal.

6   Woolworth   1970
oil on canvas 198 x 198
Collection Edward Bianchi, NYC

7   Roxy   1971/72   *Illustrated*
oil on canvas 198 x 198 –
Collection Saul P Steinberg, NYC

8   Her   1973
acrylic on paper 27 x 27
Lent by the artist

9   Keegan   1973
acrylic on paper 27 x 27
Lent by the artist

10   Taft   1973
acrylic on paper 27 x 27
Lent by the artist

11   New Jersey Central   1973
acrylic on paper 27 x 27
Lent by the artist

12   Orph   1972
lithograph 87 x 61 from *10 documenta super realists* portfolio
published by Shorewood Atelier, NYC, edition of 300
Arts Council Collection

Why do you paint signs?
I have always been fascinated with them. I can remember liking downtown areas when I was a kid, and I guess it has just followed me. I like letter forms too. I started doing buildings and gradually began to look up higher and saw things up there that nobody ever notices. Most of these signs are from the thirties and forties but I am not doing it to be nostalgic. They just happen to be the most interesting signs around – the ones with the most texture, the most activity.

Do you photograph them in bright sunlight?
I did until very recently. I find myself caring less about the sunshine and shadows and getting more into reflections on the surface and what's happening across the street and bouncing off the glass. This is an indication of what I want to do next. I kept trying to go in closer and closer with the subject, and when it got to a point where I couldn't go in anymore – it became uninteresting. Now, I have found that you can go in closer and go all the way through it and come out on the other side.

Among the New Realist painters, your work is perhaps the most obviously composed. Do you feel that your concerns are somewhat different?
Yes, but I can't get into it thoroughly because I hate to intellectualise too much about my work. I would rather let the painting do the talking. I think a lot of the realists are taking a scene and reproducing it as realistically as possible. I don't care about being realistic. In other words, I don't put in little rust spots or bolts that show. I'm not looking for that kind of realism. I'm just using the subjects as the stepping-off points to compose the painting.

Do you think the photograph transforms the subject matter?
No, the photograph doesn't. It isolates it better than looking at the building. I compose from it easier.

from an interview by Linda Chase and Ted McBurnett, *Art in America,* Nov/Dec 1972

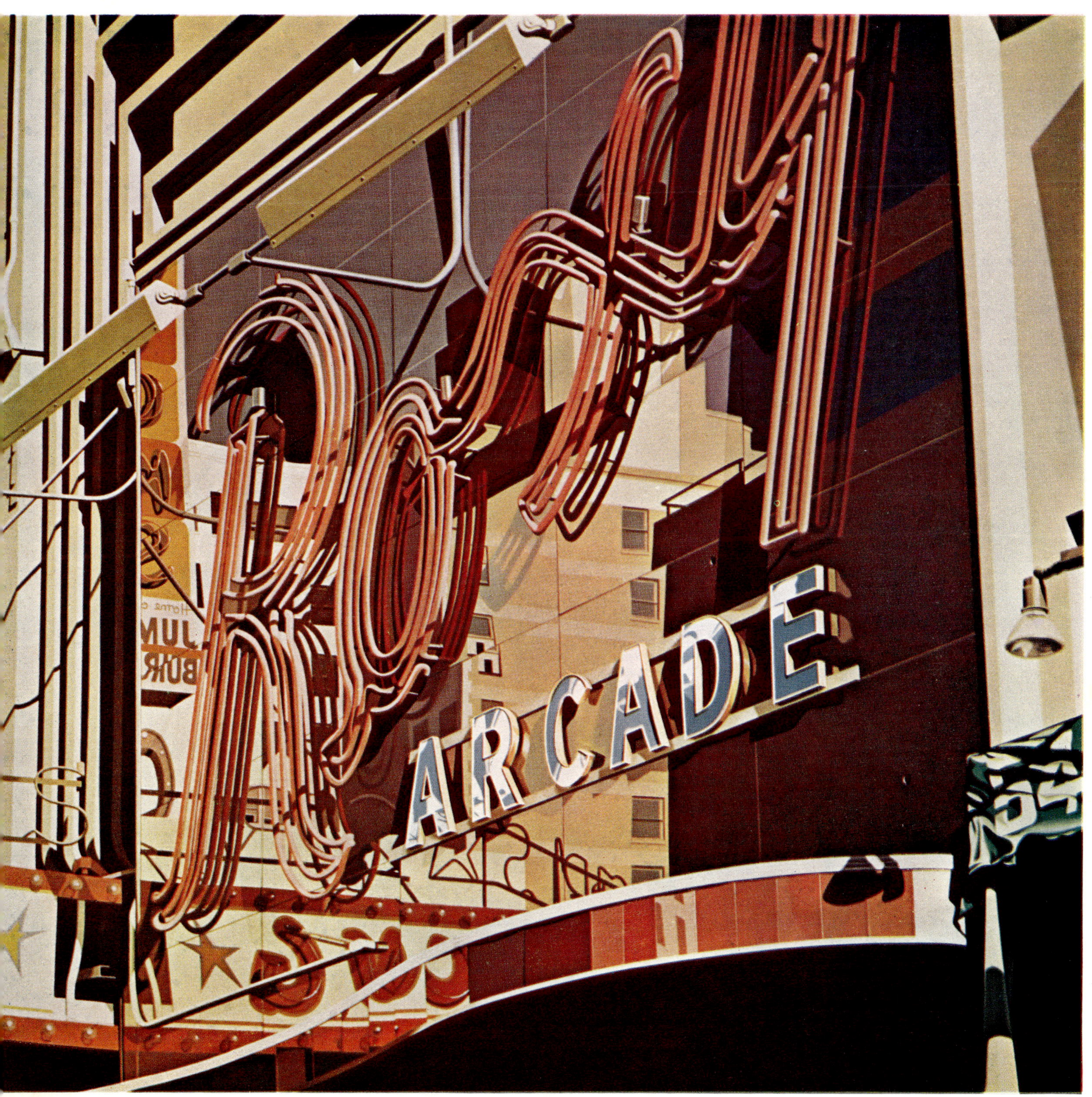
ROSY
ARCADE

Don Eddy

Born at Long Beach, California in 1944. Studied at University of Hawaii, Honolulu 1967–69 and University of California, Santa Barbara 1969–70. Lives in Santa Barbara.

One-man exhibitions 1968 Ewing Krainin Gallery, Honolulu; 1969 Crossroads Gallery, Honolulu; 1970, 1971 Molly Barnes Gallery, Los Angeles; Galerie M E Thelen, Essen and Cologne; 1971 Galerie de Gestlo, Bremen; 1972 French and Co, NYC

Some group exhibitions 1970 *7 Realisten,* Galerie Hella Nebelung, Düsseldorf; *Wirklicher als Wirklcih,* Galerie M E Thelen, Essen and Cologne; *Beyond the Actual: Contemporary Californian Realist Painting,* Pioneer Museum, Stockton, California; 1971 *Radikaler Realismus,* Galerie M E Thelen, Cologne; *New Realism,* State University at Potsdam, NY; *Neue amerikanische Realisten,* Galerie de Gestlo, Bremen; *Shape of Realism,* Deson Zaks Gallery, Chicago; *Radikaler Realismus I,* Galerie Dorothea Leonhart, Munich; *VII Biennale des Jeunes Artistes,* Paris; 1972 *Sharp-Focus Realism,* Sidney Janis Gallery, NYC; *documenta 5,* Kassel; *Hyperrealistes Americains,* Galerie des 4 Mouvements, Paris; 1972/73 *Amerikanischer Fotorealismus,* Württembergischer Kunstverein, Frankfurter Kunstverein, Kunst-und Museumsverein, Wuppertal; 1973 *Ekstrem realisme,* Louisiana Museum of Modern Art, Humlebaek

13 Untitled 1971 *illustrated*
oil on canvas 122 × 167
Ludwig Collection, Neue Galerie, Aachen

Do you work from black-and-whites or slides?
I've always worked from black-and-white. If you work from slides, you're forced to make decisions more as photographic problems than as painting problems. I found slides too restricting — whether I wanted to or not I was constantly referring back to the colour system out there which really wasn't important to me. The same was true of the balance of the painting. With slides I found I had to work out all those problems of balance out there on the street with the camera rather than in the studio.

Then you change the colours when you do the painting?
The colour system is completely related to the painting itself. When I begin the painting I have no idea what colour anything is, because I may have taken the photograph 3,000 miles away or two months before I get around to working from it, so the colour system just develops within the painting itself.

So there are only certain aspects of realism that interest you, even though the end result is realistic?
The central problem in the paintings to me is a painting problem and not a subject matter problem. It has to do with the relationship between the outside world, the surface of the canvas, and the kind of tension that is set up between illusionary space and the integrity of the surface of the canvas. What I've been working on, largely, is setting up this kind of tension so that things refer not only to reality, but also back to painting.

Where, then, does the photograph fit in?
It adds another element to that kind of special tension, because it raises the question of whether you are looking at an illusion of objects in space, or a representation of a flat piece of paper — a photograph — which is in turn a representation of things in space. So when you add the photograph in there between the things in space and the painting, the painting begins to flatten out as you think of it as a photograph and not an illusion of space. So it's important in that sense, but the idea of being photographic or true to life doesn't really interest me. It's the references between what we know, what we see, what we think we see and what's there, between the surface of the canvas and the illusion in the canvas — those are the real problems, it seems to me.

Your paintings have a greater range of focus than a photograph. Why is this?
A camera only makes two distinctions; one is focus and the other is value. Neither of these qualities in my paintings is photographic, because I take several photographs and then work from the particular one which gives me the kind of information I need for that area. I do my own developing and printing, and I can print to bring out different value scales. I also take a number of photographs that give me different focal points.

How do you choose your subject matter? Are you involved with it specifically?
I think the subject matter is dictated to me by the kind of painting problems I'm interested in. In the recent paintings of the windows I was interested in a kind of logical sequential space which was at the same time illogical and as a result both indicated space and negated space. Windows were a logical choice for this because of the unique situation they present. You can either look through the window, or at the window, or at the reflection in the window. Nobody ever looks at all three at once, because it is impossible to focus on all three. So what I do is create a space that is both logical and sequential in the sense that it is just a window space and a reflection and things through it, but at the same time I use multiple focus so that it ends up being illogical in the sense that you would not see all of these things simultaneously. The painting indicates a kind of space that is then flattened out again, because you are looking at all these things at once.

We've talked about general influences. What do you consider to be your specific influences?
Ingres. Essentially I consider myself a sort of classicist, since what I'm interested in is formal visual problems, so I relate to his work very specifically on this level. Another specific influence would be Hans Hofmann — it has to do with the way spatial tensions are set up and resolved, and colour systems. Essentially formal problems, again.

from an interview by Nancy Foote, *Art in America*, Nov/Dec 1972

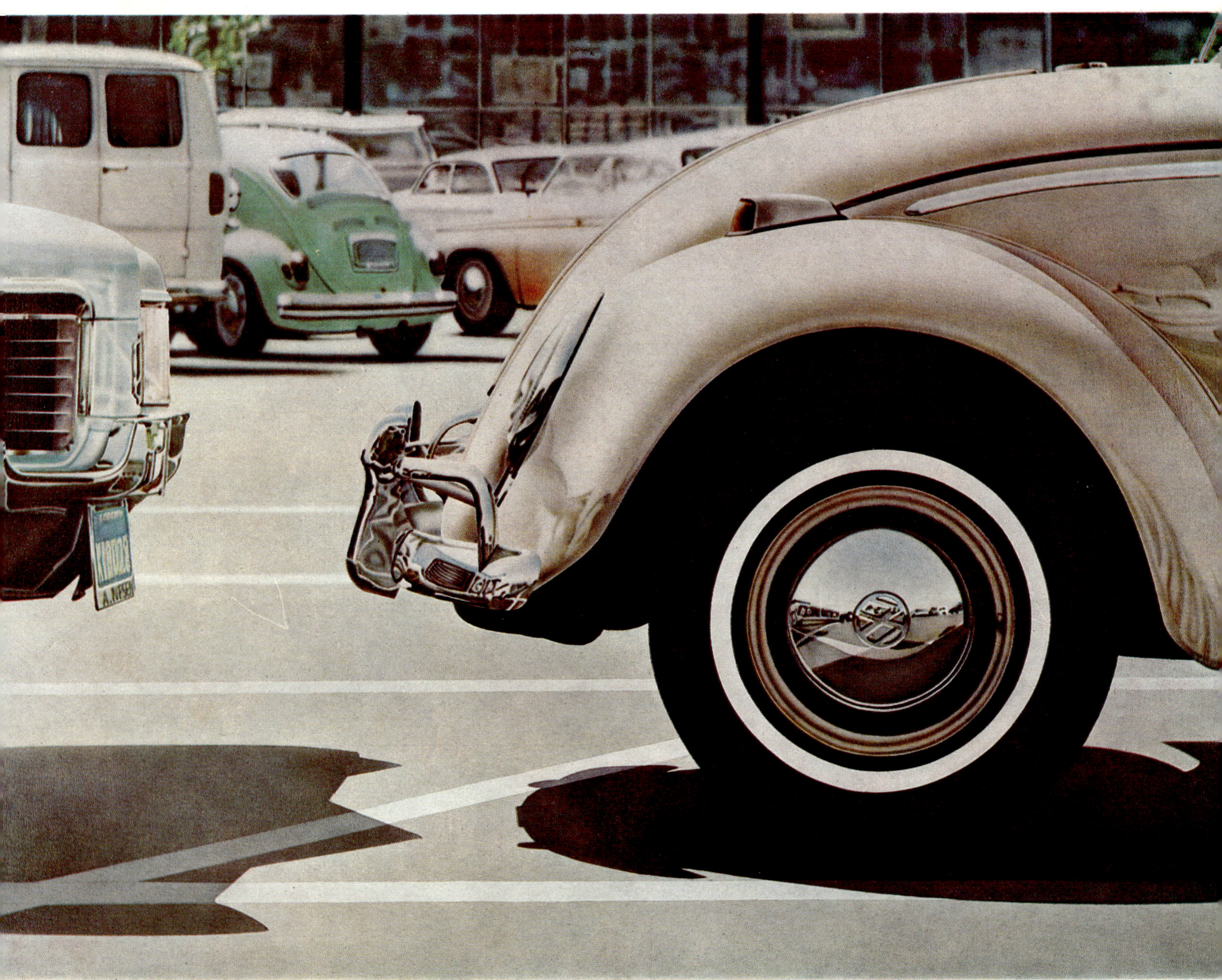

Richard Estes

Born in Evanstown, Illinois in 1936. Studied at Chicago Art Institute 1952–56. Lives in New York.

One-man exhibitions 1968 Hudson River Museum, Yonkers, NY; 1968, 1969, 1970, 1972 Allan Stone Gallery, NYC

Some group exhibitions 1968 *Survey of American Painting,* Vassar College, NY; 1969 *Aspects of a New Realism* Milwaukee Art Center, Wisconsin; 1970 *Directly Seen: New Realism in California,* Newport Harbor Art Museum, Balboa, California; *22 Realists,* Whitney Museum of American Art, NYC; *Cool Realism,* Everson Museum of Art, Syracuse, NY; *New Realism '70,* St Cloud College, Minnesota; 1971 *Neue amerikanische Realisten,* Galerie de Gestlo, Hamburg; *Radical Realism,* Museum of Contemporary Art, Chicago; 1972 *Sharp-Focus Realism,* Sidney Janis Gallery, NYC; *documenta 5,* Kassel; *documenta and no-documenta realists,* Galerie de Gestlo, Hamburg; 1972–73 *Amerikanischer Fotorealismus,* Württembergischer Kunstverein, Frankfurter Kunstverein, Kunst-und Museumsverein, Wuppertal; 1973 *Ekstrem realisme,* Louisiana Museum of Modern Art, Humlebaek

14 Food Shop 1967 *illustrated*
oil on canvas 166 x 123
Ludwig Collection, Wallraf-Richartz Museum, Cologne

15 Bus Window 1969
oil on canvas 62 x 84
Ludwig Collection, Wallraf-Richartz Museum, Cologne

16 Store Front 1971
oil on canvas 76 x 107
Collection Sydney and Frances Lewis, Richmond, Virginia

17 Bus Reflection 1972
oil on canvas 98 x 128
Collection Saul P Steinberg, NYC

18 Urban Landscape 1971
portfolio of 8 silkscreen prints published by Parasol Press, NYC with Galerie de Gestlo, Hamburg and Galeri Östergren, Malmö, edition of 75
Collection John Ward Pawson, Halifax

Would it be possible to make the same paintings from life?
You couldn't do it. It's not possible. The great thing about the photograph is that you can stop things — this is one instant. You certainly couldn't do that if you went out there and set yourself up in front of it.

How do you think your painting is affected by the photograph?
I can't see how I could do one without the other — or maybe I could do the photograph without the painting, but I couldn't do the painting without the photograph. Taking the photograph is the first step. The idea occurs and is involved with the photograph. That's the creation of it almost, and the painting is just the technique of transmitting, or finishing it up so to speak. I am not trying to enlarge the photograph. I am making a painting, basically, and just using all these other things to do it.

Are you interested in photography apart from the paintings?
No. I think I hit upon this more through photography than painting but I couldn't really carry it far enough with photography, make an object of it, shall we say. You have a little slide and that's not quite right. Slides are much nicer than prints, but it's just simply impossible to look at slides. They are too small, and if you project them they lose that quality, and if you have prints made they are too flat. It loses something — surface. There's a lot of things in painting that you have more control over than you have in a photograph. You can't just ask the people to go away so you can take a picture, or move this car over there. In a painting you can make this line a little stronger, change the depth, things like that.

Do you think New Realism is a reaction to what was going on before?
Yes, I think so. Abstract painting was a reaction to realism, and realism is a reaction to abstraction. It goes back and forth.

Many New Realists were abstract painters to begin with. Do you think that has had any effect?
They were trained that way. The kind of painting they are doing owes a lot to that kind of training. They couldn't really be doing the same kind of painting if they hadn't had that. Maybe that's what's behind the coldness of it, I don't know — a cold, abstract way of looking at things, without any comment or commitment.

Do you think that is particularly an American thing?
Yes, certain American painting has always had a kind of starkness. I think what we have here is a very raw kind of life.

Your paintings seem to have the effect of making the viewer see things differently, making the subject beautiful or interesting. Is that your intention?
I have no conscious intention of making people see differently. I don't enjoy looking at the things I paint, so why should you enjoy it? I enjoy painting it because of all the things I can do with it. I'm not trying to make propaganda for New York, or anything. I think I would tear down most of the places I paint.

Do you think it's true that beautiful things often don't make very interesting subjects?
That's true. Even if I were going to paint figures I wouldn't look for beautiful people to paint. It's interesting, it's very difficult to paint trees too. It's funny, all the things I was trained to paint — people and trees, landscapes and all that — I can't paint. We're living in an urban culture that never existed even fifty years ago.

from an interview by Linda Chase and Ted McBurnett, *Art in America* Nov/Dec 1972

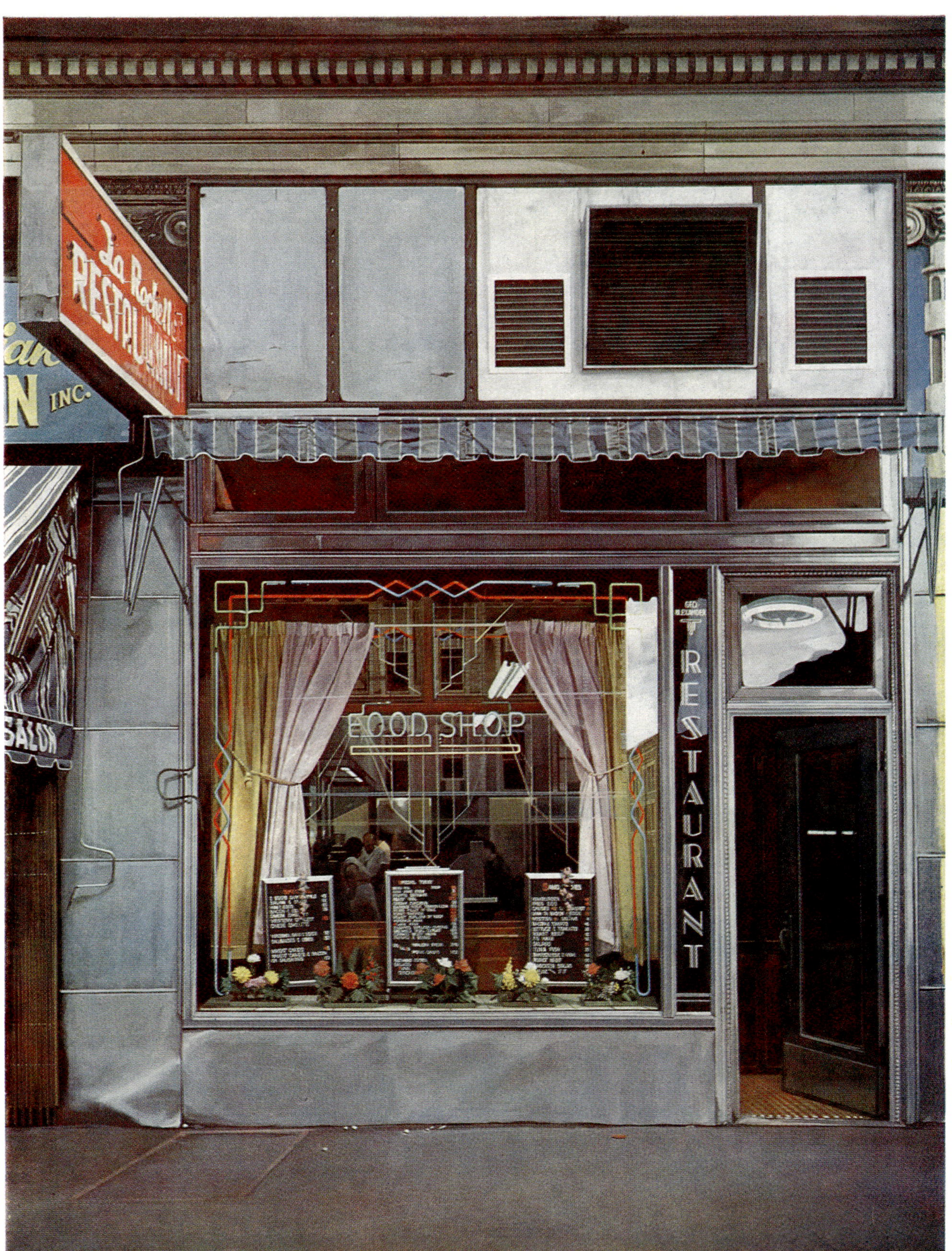

La Rochelle
RESTAURANT
INC.
SALON
FOOD SHOP
RESTAURANT
GEO. ALEXANDER

Ralph Goings

Born in Corning, California in 1928. Studied at California College of Arts and Crafts, Oakland 1950–53, and Sacramento State College 1956. Lives in Sacramento.

One-man exhibitions 1960, 1962, 1968 Artists Cooperative Gallery, Sacramento; 1966 Candy Store Gallery, Folsom California; 1970 O K Harris, NYC

Some group exhibitions 1969 *Aspects of a New Realism,* Milwaukee Art Center, Wisconsin; 1970 *The Highway Show,* Institute of Contemporary Art, Philadelphia; *The Cool Realists,* Jack Glenn Gallery, Corona del Mar, California; *Directly Seen: New Realism in California,* Newport Harbor Art Museum, Balboa, California; 1971 *Shape of Realism,* Deson Zaks Gallery, Chicago; *Radical Realism,* Museum of Contemporary Art, Chicago; *Neue amerikanische Realisten,* Galerie de Gestlo, Bremen and Hamburg; *New Realism,* State University at Potsdam, NY; 1972 *Sharp-Focus Realism,* Sidney Janis Gallery, NYC; *Phases of New Realism,* Lowe Art Museum, Coral Gables, Florida; *documenta 5,* Kassel; *documenta and no-documenta realists,* Galerie de Gestlo, Hamburg; *Hyperrealistes Americains,* Galerie des 4 Mouvements, Paris; 1972/73 *Amerikanischer Foto-realismus,* Württembergischer Kunstverein, Frankfurter Kunstverein, Kunst-und Museumsverein, Wuppertal; 1973 *Ekstrem realisme,* Louisiana Museum of Modern Art, Humlebaek

19 Airstream Trailer 1970 *illustrated*
oil on canvas 152 x 214
Ludwig Collection, Neue Galerie, Aachen

20 Untitled 1971
lithograph 57 x 73, published by O K Harris, NYC
Arts Council Collection

21 Camper 1972
lithograph 61 x 88 from *10 documenta super realists* portfolio
published by Shorewood Atelier, NYC, edition of 300
Arts Council Collection

What does the camera do to reality?
It changes some things. It also gives you access to information that you can't get any other way. The camera sees monocularly. It only has one eye and I have two, as do most artists. And when I'm looking at something directly, by shifting my head just a little bit relationships change. If there's an awkward juxtaposition, say, of two forms, the natural tendency, when drawing directly from the subject, would be to shift your head so that — in terms of traditional ideas about composition — it would be corrected. The camera doesn't make those kinds of distinctions and corrections. That's one of the things I find delightful about working from photographs. You really get a chance to see reality in all of its awkwardness, and all of its randomness. It's frozen, it's there, unchanging, once the photograph is taken. No matter how you're going to move your head, you're not going to compensate for certain overlappings or awkward combinations of things that violate traditional ideas of composition.

How important is subject matter to you?
The subject matter is what the painting is all about. I don't select it because it has dramatic compositional elements. I select it because of the specific thing that it is.

I like to render. I like to copy — I do a lot of copying — I like tracing. I trace a lot. I find that that's a very useful tool for me. But maybe what I should have said, instead of a painting problem, it's a rendering problem involved in that back window with its reflection plus the sunlight coming through plus the objects behind it. Not simply because it's reflections. I know that this has become a kind of thing, to paint reflections and reflections are a lot of fun. But all kinds of shiny things are fun to paint. I also find a good deal of pleasure in painting areas of very subdued light next to very strong areas of light. For instance, the area under a truck, where there's a very strong shadow. Sometimes I try to open this up just a little and play with those values that exist under there, because some really juicy colour can be manipulated. I think most people notice reflections because they think, wow, how did he do that. It's like some of the Dutch still-life paintings. The things that look so fantastic and wondrous were probably terrific fun to do. And they're really not all that hard.

Your paintings are very spick-and-span; that's considered a kind of Neo-Classic trait, isn't it?
It may have to do with the great deal of time involved in making the painting. Maybe the paintings would be a little more naturalistic, in the sense of kind of trashy and rough and coarse, if they were done over a period of two or three days. But where they're done over a period of forty-five to fifty days, and where one day's work — one eight or ten-hour day's work — is devoted entirely to maybe three or four square inches of canvas, the intense concentration on rendering may have this sterilising effect you mention. I'm not really conscious of it. I don't really think a lot about it. I wonder if it's because I'm very conscious of not making any kind of judgement or comment about the subject matter, other than that I think it's terrifically beautiful as a thing to paint. Now don't misunderstand that. I'm not saying that hamburger stands are inherently beautiful in themselves. It's not the object that I'm concerned with; it's the painting of the object. So perhaps in my concern for making the row of seats as beautiful as possible and the reflection on the floor as beautiful as possible, I may, inadvertently because of this, make it neater-looking than it looks in reality. Now if that's a Neo-Classic trait, I don't know.

from an interview by Brian O'Doherty, *Art in America*, Nov/Dec 1972

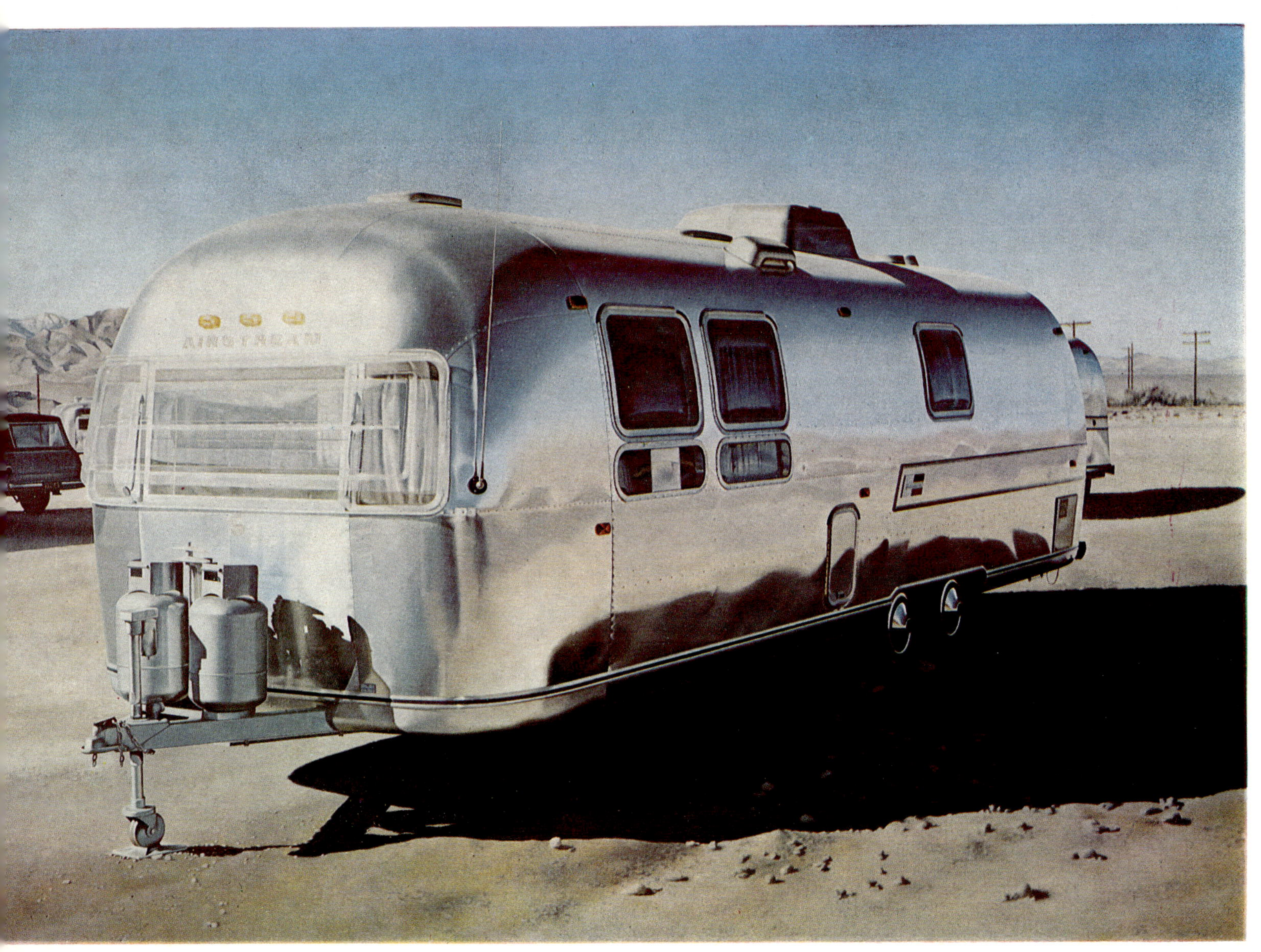

Nancy Stevenson Graves

Born in Pittsfield, Massachusetts in 1940. Studied at Vassar College 1958–61 and Yale University, School of Art and Architecture 1964. Awarded Fulbright-Hayes Scholarship to study in Paris in 1965 and lived and worked in Florence in 1966. Lives in New York.

One-man exhibitions 1968 Graham Gallery, NYC; 1969, 1971 National Gallery of Canada, Ottawa; 1969 Whitney Museum of American Art, NYC; 1971 Reese Palley Gallery, NYC; Neue Galerie, Aachen; Vassar College, NY; *Projects, Nancy Graves,* Museum of Modern Art, NYC; 1972 New Gallery, Cleveland, Ohio

Some group exhibitions 1970 *Klischee und Antiklischee,* Neue Galerie, Aachen; *Information,* Museum of Modern Art, NYC; 1971 *London Film Festival '71; Depth and Presence,* Corcoran Gallery, Washington, DC; *Prospect '71/Projection,* Kunsthalle, Düsseldorf; *Extended Structures,* Museum of Contemporary Arts, Chicago; *VI Biennale des Jeunes Artistes,* Paris; 1972 *documenta 5,* Kassel; *Prospect,* Louisiana Museum of Modern Art, Humlebaek; *American Women Artists,* Kunsthalle, Hamburg; 1973 *Ekstrem realisme,* Louisiana Museum of Modern Art, Humlebaek

22   Mongolian Bactrian dedicated to Harvey Brennan
1969   *illustrated*
wood, steel, canvas, wax, oil paint, hide and polyurethane 244 x 320 x 122
Ludwig Collection, Neue Galerie, Aachen

Letter from Martin W Cassidy, Museum of Natural History, New York

Dear Dr Becker,
Many thanks for your letter. I hope my brief comments will be useful to you. I am to some considerable extent familiar with the work of Nancy Stevenson Graves, especially where her *Bone-Sculptures* are concerned. For years I have been professionally concerned with the fossils of vertebrates, and I must say it strikes me as surprising when these sculptures are described as reproductions. I am aware that all of us, when we confront an unfamiliar event, tend to want to see only those aspects that are familiar and harmless. It is true that our first sight of these sculptures give us an overwhelming impression of their presence. Yet one recognises quite soon that it was never Miss Graves' sole intention to *reproduce* fossil remains. Not that she would lack the technical ability to achieve this — on the contrary her skills in this respect are remarkable. Only after the first strange impression of these sculptures as sheer spectacle fades, do we recognise that we are being offered artistic statements on an entirely different level — statements that go far beyond osteology. They are suggestive structural evocations leading us beyond the demonstration of the original relationships between the individual parts. Miss Graves has quite evidently also acquired a far-reaching knowledge of such exceptional areas of study as palaeontology and anthropological philosophy. It seems to be very rare these days for an artist to enlarge his understanding in this manner. Adopting the usual habit of art jargon to name only the surface, one could perhaps describe Nancy Graves as a facsimilist.
I wish you every success with your exhibition.
With best wishes,
Martin W Cassidy

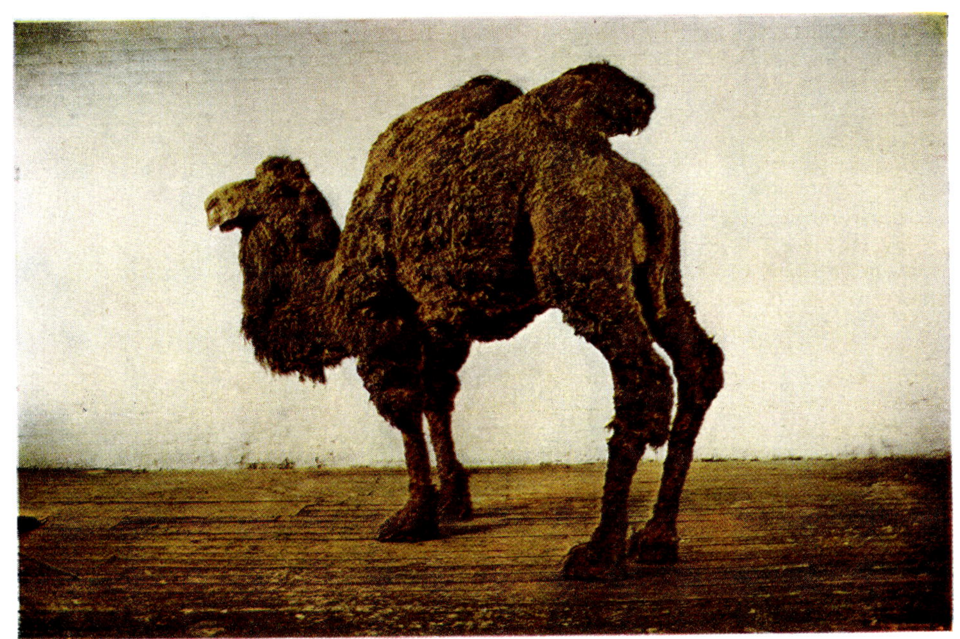

Duane Hanson

Born in Alexandria, Minnesota in 1925. Studied at Luther College, Decorah, Iowa 1943–44, University of Washington, Seattle 1944–45, Malcalester College, St Paul, Minnesota 1946 and Cranbrook Academy of Art, Bloomfield Hills, Michigan 1950–51. For sixteen years taught in Free Schools in the USA and Germany. Lives in New York.

One-man exhibitions 1951 Cranbrook Academy of Art, Bloomfield Hills, Michigan; 1952 Wilton Gallery, Wilton, Connecticut; 1958 Galerie Netzel, Bremen; Norton Gallery of Art, Palm Beach, Florida; Ringling Museum, Sarasota, Florida; 1970, 1972 O K Harris, NYC

Some group exhibitions 1969 *Human Concern: Personal Torment – The Grotesque in American Art,* Whitney Museum of American Art, NYC; 1970 *Klischee und Antiklischee,* Neue Galerie Aachen; *Figures – Environments,* Walker Art Center, Minneapolis, Minnesota; 1971 *Radical Realism,* Museum of Contemporary Art, Chicago; 1972 *Sharp-Focus Realism,* Sidney Janis Gallery, NYC; *documenta 5,* Kassel; *Phases of New Realism* Lowe Museum of Art, Coral Gables, Florida; 1973 *Ekstrem realisme,* Louisiana Museum of Modern Art, Humlebaek

23 The Supermarket Lady 1970 *illustrated*
fibreglass and clothing life-size
Ludwig Collection, Neue Galerie, Aachen

Do you feel that your sculpture or the way you think about it relates to the media or to photography?
Well, there is certain imagery that I identify with. I will see a picture in the newspaper, especially sports and action. Sometimes you see a gruesome sight like an accident or a war scene where the imagery is powerful, but if I try to copy the poses it doesn't work. I tried that once with football players and it just didn't work out, so I use the picture as a point of departure. With everyday scenes, I just imagine those.

One definition of New Realism is that it doesn't make any comment; it's objective.
Yes, that refers to the paintings. In a way I fit in and in a way I don't. New Realist painting reflects everyday life or what we are thinking about, whatever it is you recognise, imagery you are confronted with. But it's not like Pop art, it's more reserved; it's just taking it with no comment. To me that wasn't enough. I wanted to comment and was criticised that I was doing it for shock. For me, I feel that I have to identify with those lost causes, revolutions and so forth. I am not satisfied with the world. Not that I think you can change it, but I just want to express my feelings of dissatisfaction. Everybody feels dissatisfied. If the artist doesn't reflect that, if he says, 'Oh no, this doesn't exist', I don't think he is being honest. I try to be honest about what I feel myself, and what others feel, and express it. If art can't reflect life and tell us more about life, I don't think it's an art that will be lasting and durable. In other words, decoration. Something that looks nice to hang on the wall. It still gives us pleasure, but how meaningful is it? It's just the happy reflection of a world that doesn't exist. Someone asked me, 'Why don't you do something happy that reflects a world that could be instead of what is?'

from an interview by Linda Chase and Ted McBurnett, *Art in America,* Nov/Dec 1972

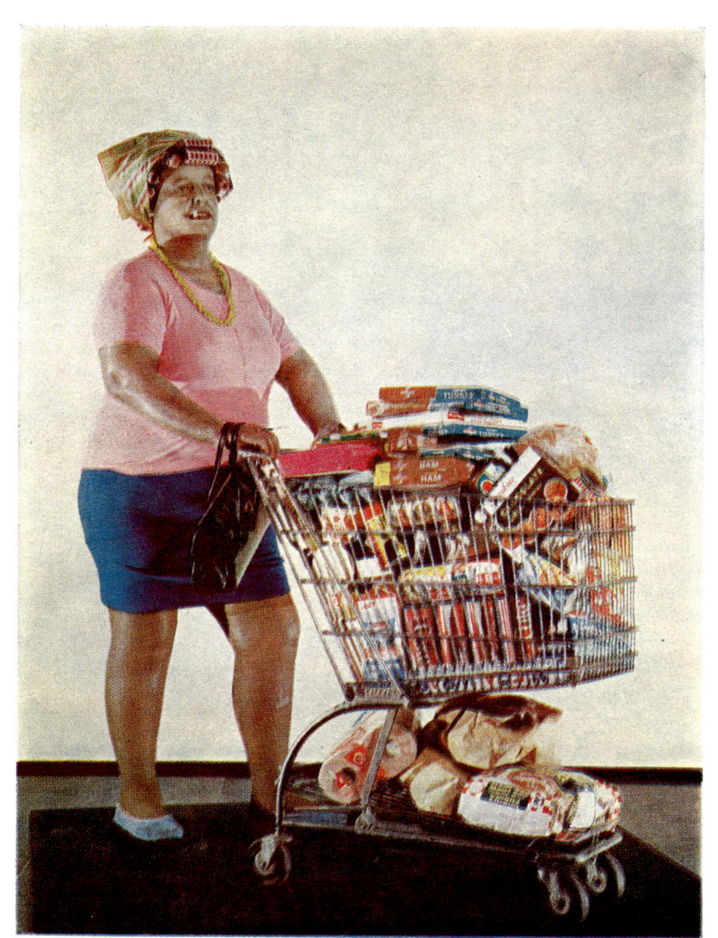

Howard Kanovitz

Born in 1929 at Fall River, Massachusetts. Studied at Providence College, Rhode Island 1947–49 and Rhode Island School of Design 1949–51. Taught at Brooklyn College and Pratt Institute, NYC 1961–64. At present lives in London.

One-man exhibitions 1962 Stable Gallery, NYC; 1964 Fall River Association, Massachusetts; 1966 Jewish Museum, NYC; 1970 Galerie M E Thelen, Cologne; Everyman Gallery, NYC; Benson Gallery, Bridgehampton, Long Island; 1971 Waddell Gallery, NYC; Galeri Östergren, Malmö; Benson Gallery, Bridgehampton, Long Island

Some group exhibitions 1968, 1969 *Critics' Choice,* State University of New York and New York State Council; 1969 *Paintings from the Photo,* The Riverside Museum, NYC; 1970 *22 Realists,* Whitney Museum of American Art, NYC; *Klischee und Antiklischee,* Neue Galerie, Aachen; *7 Realisten,* Galerie Hella Nebelung, Düsseldorf; *Wirklicher als wirklich,* Galerie M E Thelen, Cologne; 1971 *Radical Realism,* Museum of Contemporary Art, Chicago; *Kelpra Prints,* Hayward Gallery, London; *Radikaler Realismus 1,* Galerie Dorothea Leonhart, Munich; 1972 *Sharp-Focus Realism,* Sidney Janis Gallery, NYC; *Neue Realisten,* Galerie Kuckels, Bochum; *documenta 5,* Kassel; *Hyperrealistes Americains,* Galerie des 4 Mouvements, Paris; 1972/73 *Amerikanischer Fotorealismus,* Württembergischer Kunstverein, Frankfurter Kunstverein, Kunst-und Museumsverein, Wuppertal; 1973 *Ekstrem realisme,* Louisiana Museum of Modern Art Humlebaek

24   The Opening   1967
collage and plastic on perspex 49 x 69
Ludwig Collection, Wallraf-Richartz Museum, Cologne

**25   The Painting Wall
The Water Bucket Stool**   1968   *illustrated*
polymer acrylic on canvas 240 x 295 x 41
Ludwig Collection, Neue Galerie, Aachen

26   Cleo's View   1968
polymer acrylic on canvas 291 x 197 x 187
Collection Whitney Museum of American Art, NYC
Gift of the Friends of the Whitney Museum of American Art

27   Journal   1973
polymer acrylic on canvas 274 x 218
Ludwig Collection, Neue Galerie, Aachen

28   The Magazine Women Believe In   1972
lithograph 45 x 65, published by Kunstmarkt, Cologne, edition of 180
Arts Council Collection

29   Andre   1972
silkscreen 69 x 90, published by Galeri Östergren, Malmö, edition of 100
Arts Council Collection

30   Projection   1972
silkscreen 69 x 90, published by Galeri Östergren, Malmö, edition of 100
Arts Council Collection

One astonishing feature of art today is the return of a great many of today's artists from abstraction to realism. What are the reasons for this development? Is there any need for realism?
It's not surprising when you think of the various things that are happening in art. Considering modern transportation and one's resulting mobility, there are as many departures as returns and we are now beginning to realise that art exists in a state of flux, where there is a functional link between abstraction and realism. To answer the question 'is there any need for realism' I would ask 'whose need?'. The fact of its existence already proves it is necessary for some people.

Would you describe yourself as a realist?
Only when I am meditating in the marketplace (read *Be Here Now* by Baba Ram Das). But my use of a recognisable subject (is that realism?) is my way of getting close to that tough and mysterious connection between emotions and ideas — a *way* of seeing which is far from painting things as you see them. The thing is to discover what's happening in the world and when we do, perhaps that can be called realism.

The main objective of many radical realists is to translate photographic information into paint information. How do you use photographs? What do you use for this transformation?
I use photographic methods and parts of photographs as a means of synthesising images. I rarely use the whole photograph as a compositional entity. If I want to depict something in a painting, either I find a photograph of it or I take one. Often the photo contains most of the information I need to bring the painting of that thing to a conclusion. If it doesn't, I may take more photos or even do a drawing or two. To effect a transformation, you really have to plan the painting carefully.

On the whole you avoid a painterly brush stroke. Why and how?
There is no painterly brush stroke because I use an air brush which doesn't come in contact with the painting surface. The air brush has the capacity to render smooth tonal transitions and one could say that my work has an 'airy' brush stroke rather than a painterly one. The result avoids discussion of aesthetic painterliness, which to me is irrelevant.

What is 'real' in your works and what appears to be 'real'? What relationship between reality and illusion are you interested in exploring?
There is nothing in my work that isn't real, yet there is nothing real in my work but paint, canvas and stretcher. There is much though that seems to be real, and this resemblance is a way of cooling off my anxious vision; I might add — your anxious vision. The point for me is to find that stage in the painting of images that brings objects to a state of relaxed relationship to other objects, no matter how absurd, and all this should take place logically and with good sense.

The main theme of your work seems to be the relationship between reality and illusion.
In most of my paintings there is an area which is a kind of no-man's land where reality and illusion overlap. In that place, they become interchangeable. This synthetic state allows the objects to be ercognisable as both real and illusionary. Lately I've become interested in baroque illusionism, the illusion of the illusion.

Interview with Peter Sager from Magazin Kunst, XI/44 4 Quartal 1971, Alexander Baier-Press, and *documenta 5* catalogue, June 1972, Bertelsmann

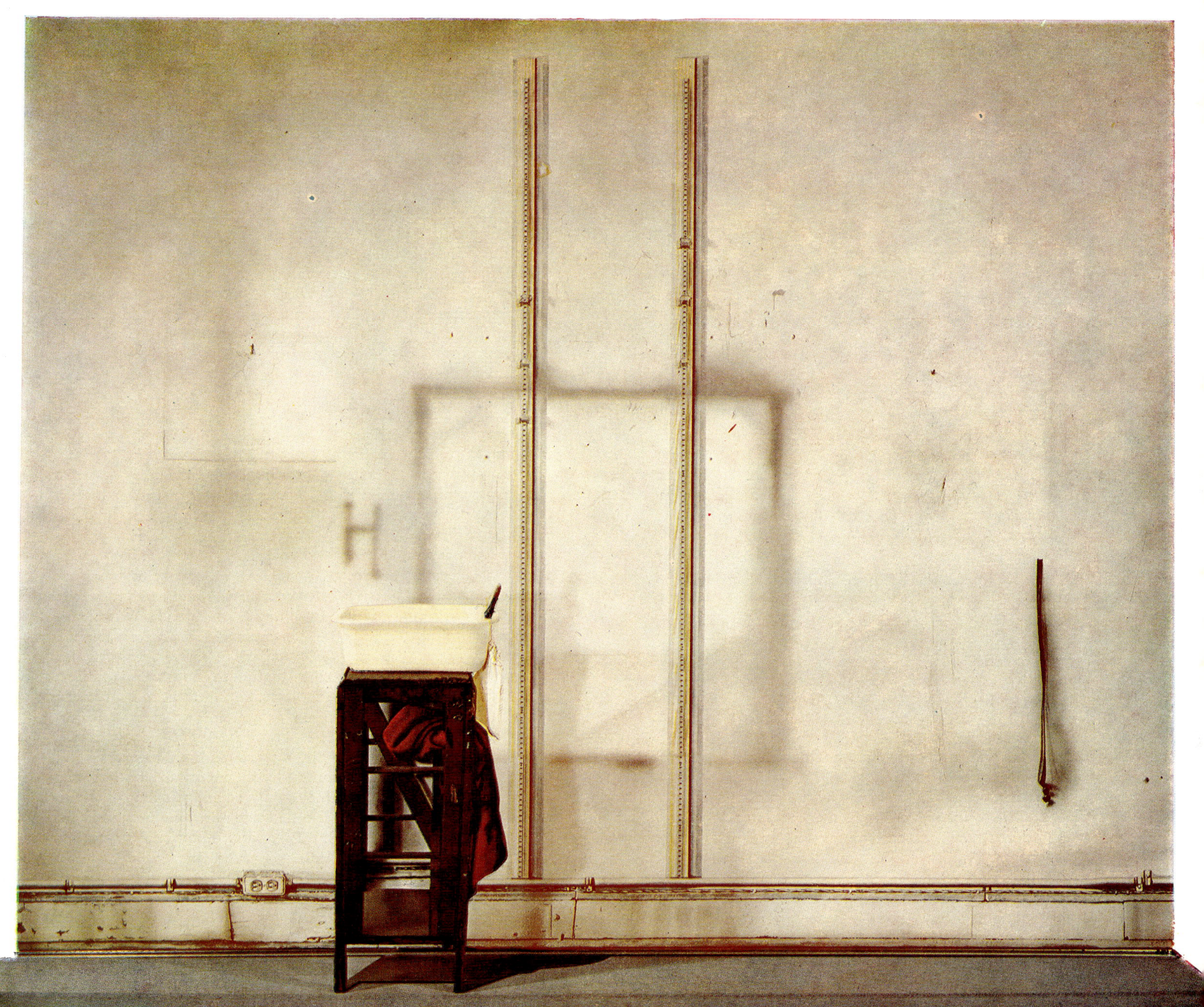

Richard McLean

Born in Hoquiam, Washington in 1934. Studied at California College of Arts and Crafts, Oakland 1955–58 and Mills College, Oakland 1960–62. Lives in San Francisco and teaches at San Francisco State College.

One-man exhibitions 1957 Lucien Labaudt Gallery, San Francisco; 1963 Richmond Art Center, California; 1964, 1966 Berkeley Gallery, California; 1965 Valparaiso University, Indiana; 1967 University of Omaha, Nebraska; 1971 O K Harris, NYC

Some group exhibitions 1966 *East Bay Realists,* San Francisco Art Institute; 1970 *People Painters,* University of California at Davis; *22 Realists,* Whitney Museum of American Art, NYC; *West Coast '70,* Crocker Art Gallery, Sacramento; *Directly Seen: New Realism in California,* Newport Harbor Art Museum, Balboa, California; *The Cool Realists,* Jack Glenn Gallery, Corona del Mar, California; *Neue amerikanische Realisten,* Galerie de Gestlo, Bremen and Hamburg; 1971 *Radical Realism,* Museum of Contemporary Art, Chicago; *New Realism,* State University at Potsdam, NY; 1972 *Sharp-Focus Realism,* Sidney Janis Gallery, NYC; *documenta 5,* Kassel; *documenta and no-documenta realists,* Galerie de Gestlo, Hamburg; *Hyperrealistes Americains,* Galerie des 4 Mouvements, Paris; 1972/73 *Amerikanischer Fotorealismus,* Württembergischer Kunstverein, Frankfurter Kunstverein, Kunst-und Museumsverein, Wuppertal; 1973 *Ekstrem realisme,* Louisiana Museum of Modern Art, Humlebaek.

31 Rustler Charger 1971 *illustrated*
oil on canvas 168 x 168
Ludwig Collection, Neue Galerie, Aachen

32 Greentree's Sloe Gin 1972
lithograph 79 x 61 from *10 documenta super realists* portfolio
published by Shorewood Atelier, NYC, edition of 300
Arts Council Collection

Out of all the photographs that are available, why did you pick ones from horse magazines?
I had done most of my early growing up in rural areas in the North-west and did a fair share of milking cows, stacking hay, riding and going to rodeos. That part of my boyhood was a very intense experience, very real, and around 1965 it began to emerge as a necessity to deal with it in some way as painting. At least it seemed to offer some rich possibilities in figurative imagery at a time when other alternatives were steadily growing less viable. I was struck with the realisation that I hadn't seen anything being done seriously, if at all, with animals in painting since Rosa Bonheur and Landseer in the last century. The abstraction of the fifties eschewed subject matter altogether, and in the sixties Pop art dealt with essentially plastic, urban symbols, and it seemed no one was painting about anything outside the city limits. Animals symbolised to me the Great Outdoors, and that particular direction appeared to me to be almost totally ignored.
Since you're going to be married to that picture for a while, you're going to be darned sure that you choose the photograph you want. What determines its suitability?
That's a difficult question to answer. I don't really know what all the ingredients are that I require of a given photograph. I have the same difficulty when I go into a store to buy some clothes and the clerk asks what I'm looking for, specifically. I have to tell her I don't know

and won't know till I see it. Sometimes I know instantly. Other times it's on a tenuous hunch, and the photo will lie around the studio for months before I decide there's a painting in it. One certain qualification the photograph must have is an absence of those qualities which would distinguish it as a work of Photographic Art. The off-the-wall reportage shot is characteristically ego-free and thus leaves you somewhere to take it as a painting.
Is the colour totally your invention?
I rely a lot on my colour sense of what's appropriate, quite apart from the source I'm looking at. So that even though I'm looking at a colour photograph, I don't precisely copy the colour I see in the photograph on to the painting. I still make adjustments. In most cases the colour is more hyped up in my painting than it is in the photograph. So I don't really even worry about whether the colours in the painting are matching the colours from the photo source too much I invent it as I go along, and if deviations happen, I go on making adjustments to compensate for those deviations along the way, so it comes out even in the end.
Were you influenced by Pop art?
Sure, I owe a big debt to Pop; but, although Pop turned me on to subject matter, it was obvious I had to find some other way of treating it which circumvented the sensationalism and some of the more clamorous excesses of Pop. I had to deal with cooler situations to begin with and then paint them in a matter-of-fact manner which would stress primarily visual values. I think, however, my stuff still has in it a quality of perversity that I grew to appreciate in Pop.
I implied earlier that my early experiences with farm life in the Land of the Big Sky accounted for what might seem to be a positive predisposition toward Western subjects, animals and people in outdoor environments. The truth is, a lot has gone down since I said goodbye to all that rather abruptly twenty years ago. Sometimes I think it was a movie I saw once. And it's precisely that estrangement, that by-now alienated distance, that gives the horse and its people their fascination as painting subjects. I don't want to know any more about them than what I've already forgotten.
Are you in search of a neutral subject?
Yes, I think neutrality is extremely important, because then the situation becomes germinal; various conclusions or readings are more apt to grow out of it. Maybe my paintings succeed when they do because some look at them and think they are humorous, others think they are biting, ripping satire, and others see them quite the way I intended.

from an interview by Brian O'Doherty, *Art in America*, Nov/Dec 1972

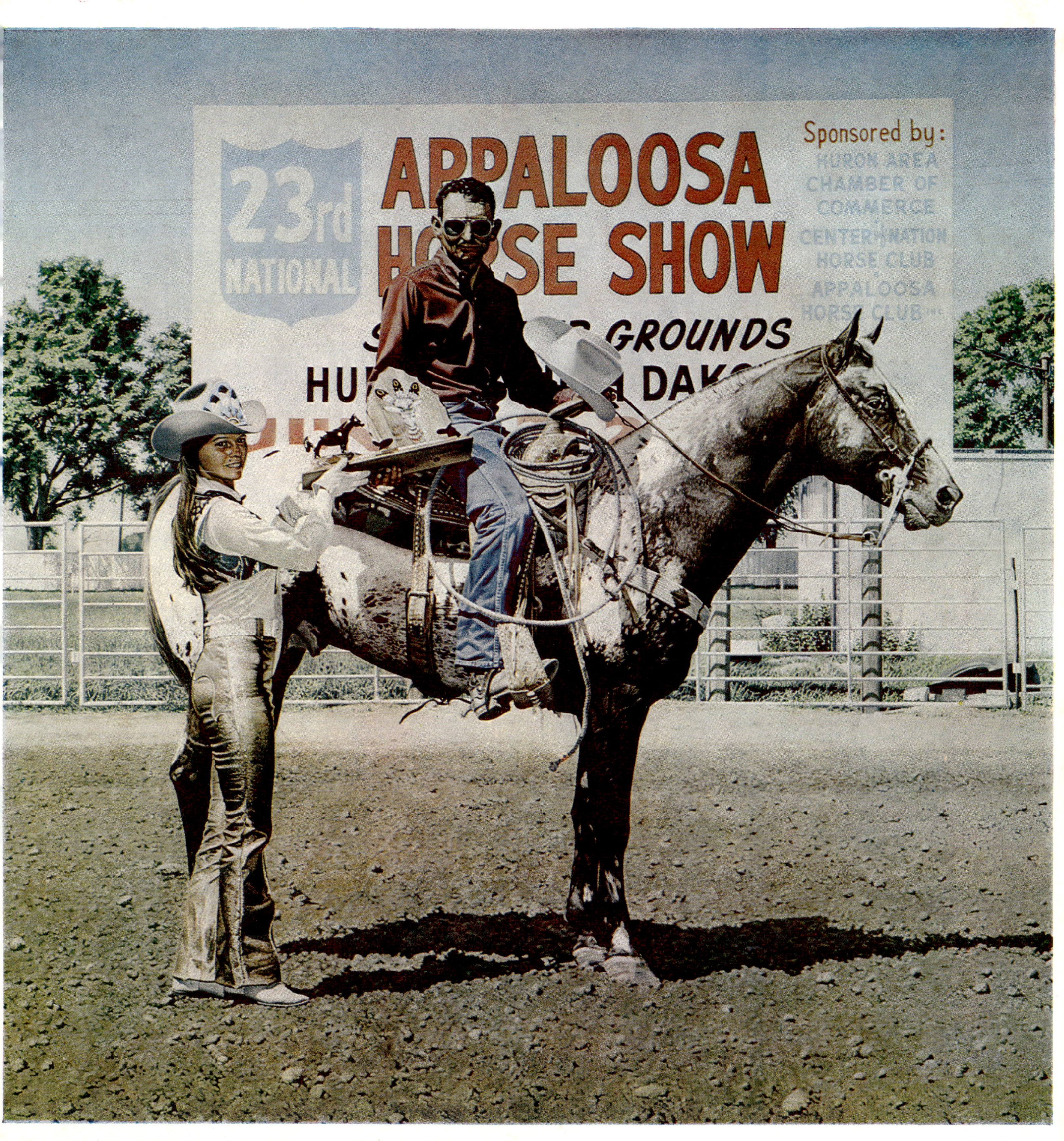

23rd NATIONAL
APPALOOSA HORSE SHOW
GROUNDS
HU DAKO
Sponsored by:
HURON AREA CHAMBER OF COMMERCE
CENTENNIAL NATION HORSE CLUB
APPALOOSA HORSE CLUB INC

Malcolm Morley

Born in London in 1931. Studied at Camberwell School of Arts and Crafts 1952–53 and the Royal College of Art 1954–56. Lectured at Ohio State University 1965–66 and School of Visual Arts, NYC 1967–69. Lives in New York and teaches at Stony Brook University, Long Island.

One-man exhibitions 1964, 1967, 1969 Kornblee Gallery, NYC

Some group exhibitions 1955 *London Group;* 1956, 1957 *Young Contemporaries,* London; 1967 *The Photographic Image,* Solomon R Guggenheim Museum, NYC; 1969 *Aspects of a New Realism* Milwaukee Art Center, Wisconsin; *Paintings from the Photo,* The Riverside Museum, NYC; 1970 *22 Realists,* Whitney Museum of American Art, NYC; *The Cool Realists,* Jack Glenn Gallery, Corona del Mar, California; 1971 *Neue amerikanische Realisten,* Galerie de Gestlo, Bremen and Hamburg; *Shape of Realism,* Deson Zaks Gallery, Chicago; *Radical Realism,* Museum of Contemporary Art, Chicago; 1972 *Sharp-Focus Realism,* Sidney Janis Gallery, NYC; *documenta 5,* Kassel; 1972/73 *Amerikanischer Fotorealismus,* Württembergischer Kunstverein, Frankfurter Kunstverein, Kunst-und Museumsverein, Wuppertal; 1973 *Ekstrem realisme,* Louisiana Museum of Modern Art, Humlebaek

33 Central Park   1970
oil on canvas 183 x 183
Ludwig Collection, Neue Galerie, Aachen

34 Race Track   1970   *illustrated*
acrylic on canvas 175 x 220
Ludwig Collection, Neue Galerie, Aachen

35 St. John's Yellow Pages   1971
oil on canvas 159 x 137
Ludwig Collection, Wallraf-Richartz Museum, Cologne

36 Horses   1969
silkscreen 70 x 78, published by Bernard Jacobsen, edition of 75
Arts Council Collection

In his paintings of the last seven years, Malcolm Morley has concentrated on structural elements. The divided picture surface as screen – this and other processes appeared so powerful as organisational strategies that Morley names them 'infinity-machine'. He divides and cuts up the picture he intends to paint into small rectangles; each rectangle is turned through 180°, and so also is the squared canvas. In this way every pre-existing meaning shatters on the illegibility of the initial situation. In return for this, the rectangles acquire qualities that invite the addition of colour. Morley can recognise a small plane with one glance, and thus creates adjacent centres that distribute themselves equivalently over the whole picture surface as though self-impelled.

The screen became a sort of universal, receptacle capable of bringing into mutual adjustment a complexity of multi-level impulses. Morley finds pictorial possibilities everywhere – in the refuse of the gutter, in a piece of woven cloth, a calendar, on the cover of a telephone directory, in a postcard – capable of translation into painting.

'I paint the world piecemeal,' says Morley, 'transforming indecision back into art. Everything is useful, everything is a suitable subject for art.'

Morley coats his canvas. He applies his colour in thick slices. Like a bricklayer with mortar he works with a sort of painter's choreography, as in the painting *Los Angeles Yellow Pages.* Iconographic meaning appears not circuitously via a contour, but as a by-product of chromatic contrast.

Morley has separated anatomy from illusion. Because for him reality is illusion. Colour patches on his canvas are fantasised by the spectator into forming a picture. Plasticity is the metaphorical correlative: colour, the plastic substance. Morley does not only show the world as painting, he shows it in a new guise. Seen close to, his picture dissolves into painting. The eye wallows in the paint surface, assembled out of registered and intact gestures. Some picture surfaces wriggle and ripple like armies of fleeing ants. It is Morley's intention to paint painting itself, to grab our eye-balls. If the brain thinks it can recognise divisions and hierarchies of figures, it is frustrated from doing so through the absence of figures. The whole canvas is the figure, and this sets up an optical pulse, since different places demand the attention of a conceptualising memory.

Morley takes the whole of art history as his empire. Art is for him the language that describes the nature of existence. And he has literally widened his language by separating out a territory that lies anterior to the word, a vacuum with an infinity of nameless qualities and countless possibilities.

Frances Morley, *documenta 5* catalogue, June 1972, Bertelsmann

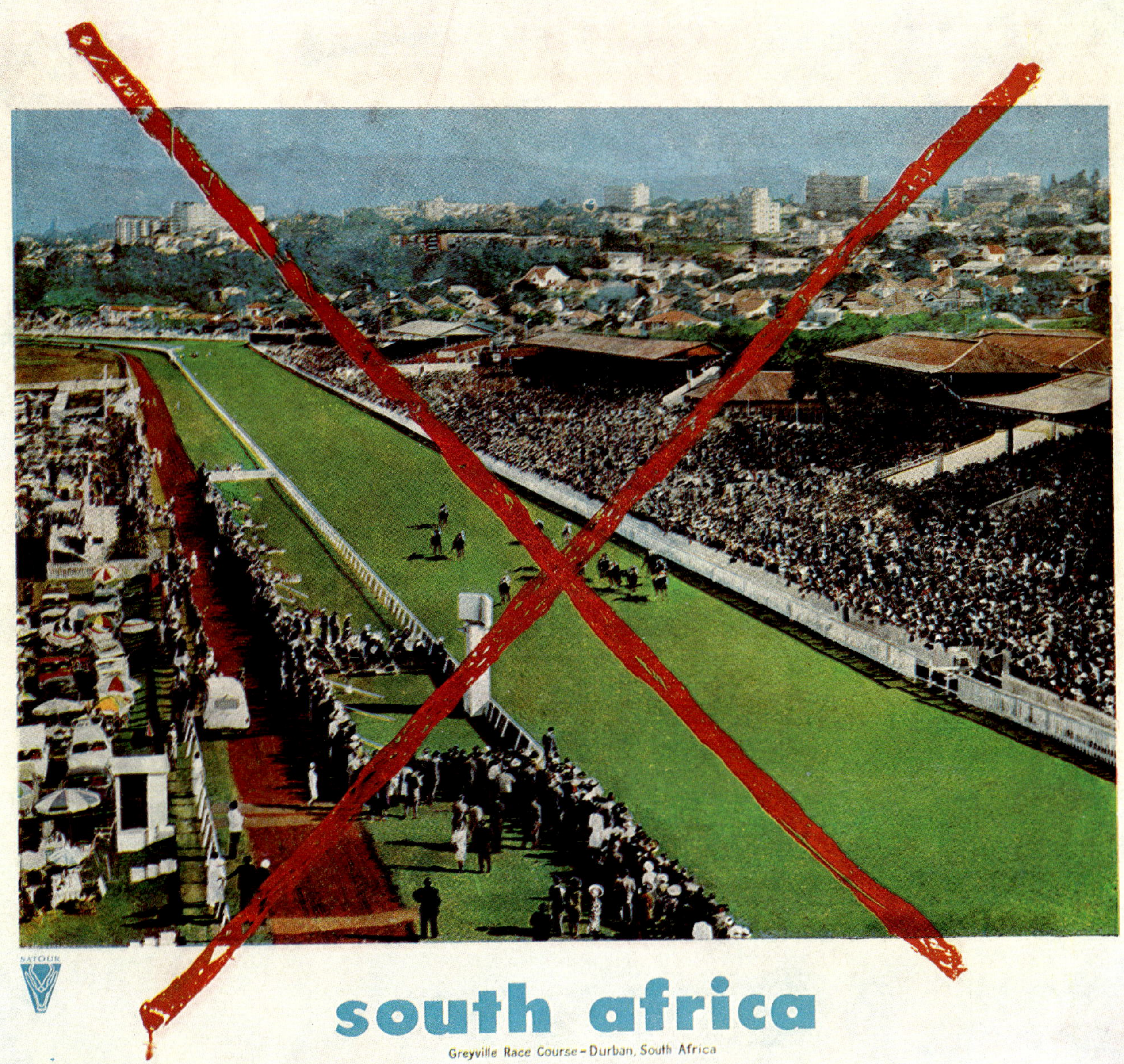
SATOUR
south africa
Greyville Race Course – Durban, South Africa

John Salt

Born in Birmingham in 1937. Studied at Birmingham College of Art 1954–57 and the Slade School of Fine Art 1958–60. Lives in New York.

One-man exhibitions 1965, 1967 Ikon Gallery, Birmingham; 1966 Lion Gallery, Stourbridge; Birmingham University; 1969 Zabriskie Gallery, NYC; 1970 Gertrude Kasle Gallery, Detroit; O K Harris, NYC; 1972 Galerie de Gestlo, Hamburg

Some group exhibitions 1970 *The Cool Realists,* Jack Glenn Gallery, California; 1971 *Radical Realism,* Museum of Contemporary Art, Chicago; *Shape of Realism,* Deson Zaks Gallery, Chicago; *VII Biennale des Jeunes Artistes,* Paris; 1972 *Relativerend Realisme,* Stedelijk van Abbemus, Eindhoven; *Sharp-Focus Realism,* Sidney Janis Gallery, NYC; *documenta 5,* Kassel; *Hyperrealistes Americains,* Galerie des 4 Mouvements, Paris; 1972/73 *Amerikanischer Foto-realismus,* Württembergischer Kunstverein, Frankfurter Kunstverein, Kunst-und Museumsverein, Wuppertal; 1973 *Ekstrem realisme* Louisiana Museum of Modern Art, Humlebaek

37 Cars 1971 *illustrated*
oil on canvas 185 x 125
Ludwig Collection, Neue Galerie, Aachen

38 Truck 1972
oil on canvas 157 x 234
Collection Armand Ornstein

39 Desert Wreck 1972
lithograph 90 x 63 from *10 documenta super realists* portfolio
published by Shorewood Atelier, NYC, edition of 300
Arts Council Collection

Do you think the photograph is of any other importance aside from the fact that it's easier? Do you think it affects the vision?
Yes, if I took a photograph of that chair and painted it, and then if I got a canvas in here and painted the chair, it would be two different things. It's like having an interpreter or transcription. I like what the photograph gives me. It's a big anti-romantic. I prefer it to painting from reality.
It gives you distance?
Yes. The trouble with painting from the object is that you might fall in love with some part of it. Also, the photo puts it all on a two-dimensional surface. That's the hard part — to go from three dimensions to two dimensions.
What about choice of subject matter?
Choice of subject matter was so obvious when I came here. The automobile was very obvious, so ugly and useless and so big, and I just got interested in it. I would never have done cars in England. It's just not that important over there. But I don't paint them because they are important or because they have some kind of message. It's just very obvious subject matter. Also, the way I was painting, using spray and air brush — that related to the way the cars are painted. They're sprayed too. I don't think the subject matter should be very important, but it is important.
What do you think of when you think of New Realism?
I think of people who work from photographs. People who work in a non-compositional or non-art way. It's like I said, the photograph wipes out art history for you. It lets you see reality before art history was invented.

from an interview by Linda Chase and Ted McBurnett, *Art in America* Nov/Dec 1972

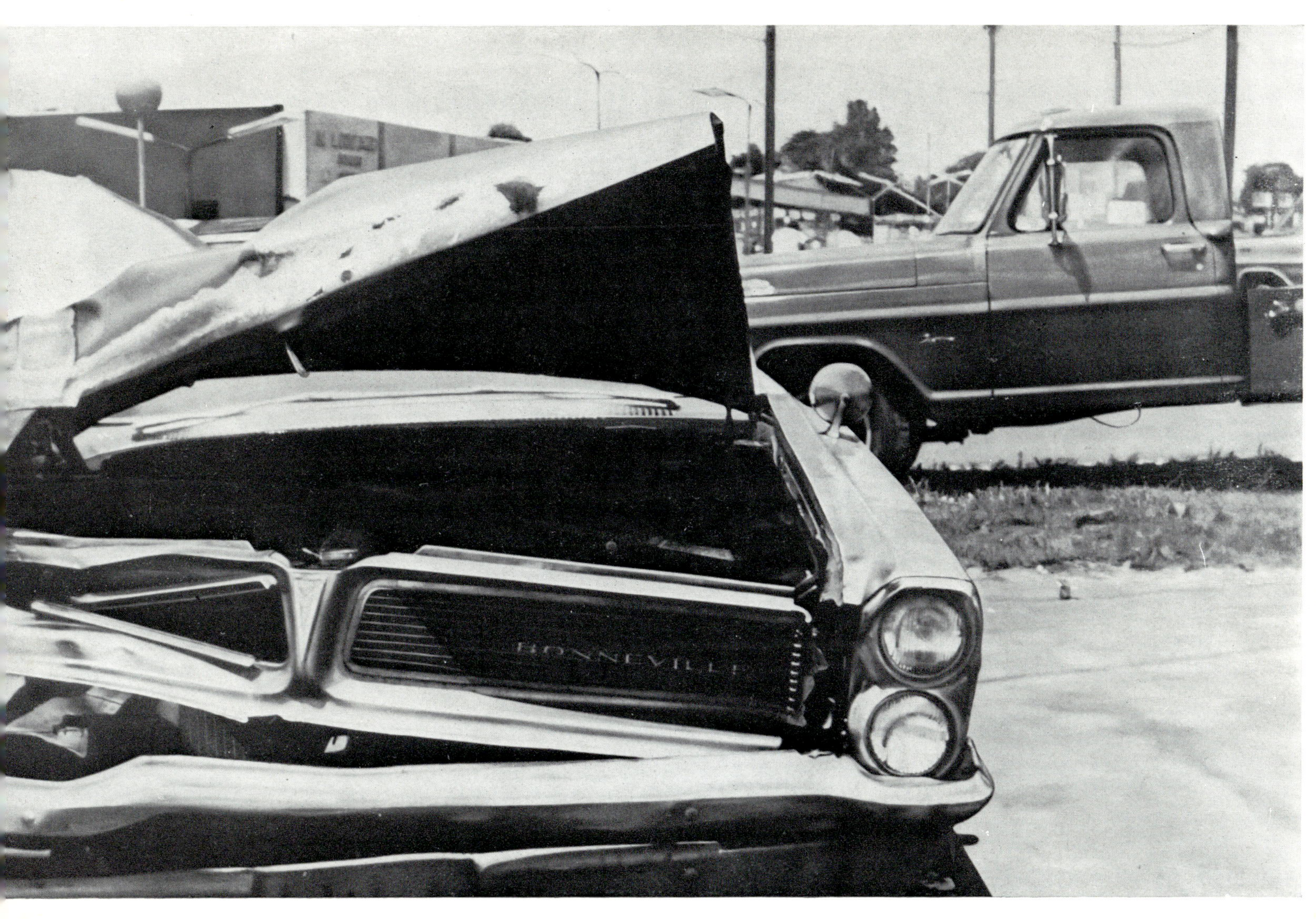
BONNEVILLE

General bibliography

Articles

Sidney Tillim, *A Variety of Realisms,* Artforum VII/10 1969

Cindy Nemser, *Sculpture and the New-Realism,* Arts Magazine, April 1970

Peter Sager, *Neue Formen des Realismus,* Magazine Kunst, 4 Quartal 1971

Robert Hughes, *The Realist as Corn God,* Time Magazine, 21 January 1972

Ivan Karp, *Rent is the Only Reality or, The Hotel instead of the Hymn,* Arts, January 1972

Barbara Rose, *Real, Realer, Realist,* New York Magazine, 31 January 1972

Henry Gerrit, *The Real Thing,* Art International, vol XVI No 6/7 1972

Felix Zdenek, *Wirklichkeit und Illusion oder: Vom Realismus zum Fotorealismus,* Kunstnachrichten, October/November 1972

Art in America, November/December 1972

Books and publications

Nicholas and Elena Calas, *Icons and Images of the Sixties,* E R Dutton & Co, NYC 1961

John Russell and Suzy Gablik, *Pop Art Redefined,* Thames & Hudson, London 1969

Michael Compton, *Pop Art,* Hamlyn, London 1970

The Pop Image of Man, Kodansha Ltd, Tokyo 1971

Art Now, New Age, Kodansha Ltd, Tokyo 1972

Udo Kultermann, *Radical Realism,* Mathews Miller Dunbar, London 1972

documenta 5 catalogue, Bertelsmann, Kassel 1972

John de Andrea
Selected articles and reviews

John Canaday, *Downtown Review,* The New York Times, 20 November 1971; John Perreault, *Downtown is Uptown, not 10th St,* Village Voice, 2 December 1971; Emily Genauer, *Art in the Artist,* The New York Post, 11 December 1971; *Look Twice,* The Art Gallery Magazine, January 1972

Robert Bechtle
Selected articles and reviews

K G Nilson, *Realism USA,* Konstrevy 2/1969; Tracy Atkinson and John Lloyd Taylor, *Likenesses,* Art and Artists, February 1970; *Review,* Artforum, April 1969; Lawrence Alloway, Arts, April 1970; Barry Lord, *The Eleven O'Clock News in Colour,* Artscanada, June 1970; Bruce Wolmer, Art News, February 1972; Carter Ratcliff, Art International, February 1972

Chuck Close
Selected articles and reviews

Cindy Nemser, *Presenting Charles Close,* Art in America, January/February 1970; John Perreault, *Chuck Close,* Village Voice, 12 March 1970; Hilton Kramer, *A New Realism Emerges,* The New York Times, 21 December 1971; Hilton Kramer, *Stealing the Modernist Fire,* The New York Times, 26 December 1971; John Perreault, *Reports, Forecasts, Surprises & Prizes,* Village Voice, 6 January 1972; John Perreault, *Art: A Lollapalooza of a Mishmash,* Village Voice, 10 February 1972

Robert Cottingham
Selected articles and reviews

Time Magazine, 21 February 1969; Artforum, September 1970; Art in America, September/October 1971; Arts Magazine, September/October 1971; Christian Science Monitor, 16 November 1971; Art International, 20 November 1971; Arts Magazine, December 1971; Arts Magazine, March 1972

Don Eddy
Selected articles and reviews

Art News, March 1970; Artforum, May 1970; The Art Gallery Magazine, June 1971; Arts Magazine, September/October 1971; *L'Hyperrealisme,* Opus International, 28 November 1971; Art News, January 1972; Arts Magazine, February 1972; Artforum, March 1972

Richard Estes
Selected articles and reviews

Rosalind Constable, *Style of the Year: The Inhumanists,* New York Magazine, 16 December 1968; *The Flowering of the Super-Real,* The New York Times, 2 March 1969; Tracy Atkinson, Art and Artists, February 1970; Rosalind E Krauss, Artforum, May 1971; Viola Herms Draht, *The 32nd Corcoran Biennial, Art as Visual Event,* Art International XV/5 May 1971; Dore Ashton, *New York Commentary: Realism Again?* Studio International, March 1972

Ralph Goings
Selected articles and reviews

Bill Marvel, *The Art Picture: Photos, Trucks, Blood — These are Galleries?* The National Observer, 5 October 1970; Jean-Louis Bourgeois, *New York Reviews,* Artforum, November 1970; Dave Hickey, *New York Reviews: Sharp-Focus Realism at Janis,* Art in America, March/April 1972; Denise Wolmer, *In the Galleries,* Arts Magazine, March 1972

Nancy Stevenson Graves
Selected articles and reviews

Robert Hughes, *Art: Out of the Junkyard,* Time Magazine, 4 January 1971; Hilton Kramer, *Downtown Scene: A Display of Bones,* The New York Times, 19 January 1971; John Perreault, *Camels,* Village Voice, 4 February 1971; Barbara Catoir, *Interview mit Nancy Graves,* Das Kunstwerk 3/XXIV May 1971; Gregory Battcock, *Celluloid Sculptors,* Art and Artists, October 1971; Jean Sutherland Boggs, *National Gallery of Canada,* Thames & Hudson 1971; Barbara Rose, New York Magazine, 17 January 1972; *Nancy Stevenson Graves, Sculpture, Drawings, Films* 1969–71, K. G. Lohse, Frankfurt 1971

Duane Hanson
Selected articles and reviews

New, Sites for New Sights, New York Magazine, 12 January 1970; *Portrait of the Artist as a Wet Hen,* Esquire, April 1970; Cindy Nemser, *Sculpture and the New Realism,* Arts Magazine, April 1970; *Presenting Duane Hanson,* Art in America, September 1970; *The New New York Naturalists,* Art International, 20 April 1971; *Duane Hanson,* Earth, August 1971; Harold Rosenberg, *The Art World: Reality Again,* The New Yorker, 5 February 1972; Henry Gerrit, *The Soho Body Snatcher,* Art News, March 1972

Howard Kanovitz
Selected articles and reviews

B H Friedman, *Focus as Physical Reality,* Art News 65/66 October 1966; *Realer than Real,* Time Magazine, 16 August 1968; Rosalind Constable, *Style of the Year: The Inhumanists,* New York Magazine,